"In *A Thousand Little Mome*
diverse history of his relation
God's wisdom to create a bool
Stories and Scriptures illustra
Read this book yourself and give as a gift."

—Robert Whitlow, best-selling author of *Relative Justice*

"As parents, we can often walk around with a great deal of guilt for a variety of reasons. *A Thousand Little Moments* is one of those books that guards the reader from that. This is due to James's pastoral heart and the biblical wisdom he passes along. Reading this book will remind you that you're not alone in your struggles as a parent. You will also be reminded of the faithfulness of our own Father in the midst of our struggles."

—John Perritt, Director of Resources for Reformed Youth Ministries, author, host of *The Local Youth Worker* podcast, father of five

"As a pastor who has been devoted to shepherding parents in how to meet the enormous challenge of leading their families, I have always been surprised by how few thoughtful, thorough, and accessible resources there are for Christian believers. In *A Thousand Little Moments*, Dickson helps remedy that deficit. Uncharacteristic for this topic, his counsel is refreshingly non-formulaic, yet still filled with eminently practical, biblical truth that is probably best read at the kitchen table. Dickson's pastor's heart shines through on every page as he becomes both coach and fellow traveling companion in the high privilege we call being a parent. I recommend this work highly."

—Rev. Dr. Thomas C. Gibbs, president, Covenant Theological Seminary

"*A Thousand Little Moments* overflows with refreshing life-won prudence. This practical, loving approach to parenting offers a fresh look at apologetics combined with biblical principles about raising children. I highly recommend it to anyone interested in laughing aloud, applying scripture to their circumstances, and learning how to be a better person while parenting. Sharing insightful, humorous, and poignant stories from his life and the lives of other relatives, Dickson imparts wise advice on solving common familial problems and challenges. Every family will benefit from reading James Dickson's powerful new book."

—Katherine Hutchinson-Hayes, EdD, author of *God's Little Black Dress for Women* and *A Fifth of the Story*

"James Dickson has creatively brought to the readers of this volume a somewhat different approach to Christian parenting. Most books and conferences give three to seven broad-ranging principles and Pastor Dickson presents a different scenario in that parenting is perhaps best understood as biblical faithfulness in "a thousand little moments." This premise is more than interesting, it is intriguing and informative not only because of his approach but because of his faithfulness to the Bible as the touchstone for effective Christian parenting. Enjoy."

—Harry L. Reeder III, Senior Pastor, Briarwood Presbyterian Church, Birmingham, Alabama

"*A Thousand Little Moments* is a hands-on book about Christian parenting. Yet it is so much more. Saturated with scriptural application and steeped in practical advice, James Dickson gets right to the point. Once you read it, you will be not only motivated but also equipped to become a better parent."

—Dr. Ryan F. Whitley, Senior Pastor, CrossPoint Church, Trussville, Alabama

JAMES DICKSON

a
thousand
little
moments

Grace-Shaped Parenting

BIRMINGHAM, ALABAMA

A Thousand Little Moments

Brookstone Publishing Group
An imprint of Iron Stream Media
100 Missionary Ridge
Birmingham, AL 35242
IronStreamMedia.com

Library of Congress Control Number: 2023900926

Cover design by Jonathan Lewis / Jonlin Creative

ISBN: 978-1-949856-89-7 (paperback)
ISBN: 978-1-949856-90-3 (eBook)

1 2 3 4 5—27 26 25 24 23

Anna, you are my helper and the love of my life.

For Pierce, Blair, and Stuart.
Mom and I delight in you!

Contents

CHAPTER 1

A Picture Is Worth a Thousand Moments

"Turn the camera off!" Thankful those were the *only* words I shouted, I wiped a bead of sweat from my forehead and bent over my newborn son, Pierce. While giving him his first bath, I'd lost control. Regret flooded in. Again. With shaking hands, my wife, Anna, and I tried to console our soapy baby. *What's wrong with me, Lord? Why can't I control a newborn and my temper? How could I yell at my mother-in-law like that?*

Our firstborn, Pierce, was days old. During his short life, I'd encountered several firsts. I had installed my first car seat, changed my first diaper, burped my first baby, and dressed my first circumcision wound—none of which came naturally. When Anna and I attempted Pierce's first bath, we naively believed it'd be a great idea to record the event.

Imagine three adults and an infant crammed in our minuscule bathroom. While my mother-in-law operated the camera, we began our work. Pierce hated his bath because we had no idea what we were doing. When our sweet son began screaming at an ear-splitting volume, my anxiety and my anger rose. I experienced emotions I'd never associated with being a new parent.

I had a sweet image of what our new family life would be like, complete with smiles and laughter. I would be a calm and comforting presence for my wife and son. I would always be in control of situations. Yet, the moment I demanded my mother-in-law stop recording Pierce's bath revealed that I would have to reimagine my vision of parenting.

Does any of this sound familiar? Deep down, we, as parents, want to know we're not alone. Guess what? We aren't alone! Each of us has failed. Most of us have had those moments we dearly wish we could take back. Many of us have some stories we'd prefer never to share. But if we did, we would quickly find a partner coming alongside us to say, "Me too."

Yes, there's comfort in being in the company of fellow parenting failures. But our shortcomings point us to the universal truth that we need Jesus. That's right. Parents need the Savior.

Why did I get angry at that moment with my son? Part of it was that I believed I would have the perfect child. Be honest. So did most of us. The expectations we place on our children are laughable, but so are the expectations we place on ourselves. We are untrained parents trying to raise little human beings.

My hot forehead that afternoon many years ago had little to do with the Georgia summer weather. It had everything to do with my desire for control, my lack of knowledge, and, ultimately, my pride. Pride is the root of all sin. It is the desire to be master over our destiny, and in the case of parenting, the master over our children's destiny.

My clumsiness during that first bath time was just the beginning. I thought I needed to learn how to care for my son's hygiene. But I needed to be taught patience. I needed to learn to listen. After all, the nurses in the hospital demonstrated how to bathe my son, but I barely paid attention. I'd muttered to myself, "How hard can it be? I've got this." The truth was, before I could train my son, I needed to be trained in one of the most foundational skills of the heart—listening.

Looking back at my parenting mistakes from years ago to those more recent, I am amazed at what God is doing in my children's lives. Maybe that is the whole point. God is the one who is building and shaping them, just as He is making and shaping me. Through our family relationships, my devotional life, my vocational life, and the work of the Holy Spirit, God has been transforming, and continues to transform, my children and me more and more into the image of Christ.

I don't have this parenting thing figured out. My wife and I are on a journey, learning what it means to lovingly shepherd the hearts of our children. We are learning, though, as our Father shepherds our hearts. Before we became parents, we were children of God, redeemed by His Son. This awareness of His loving and gracious fathering of me is the foundation behind my understanding of how I am to father my children. That is our journey, and I'd like to invite you to join in.

We need to ask ourselves a question before we begin our journey. Where are we going? After all, scripture calls us to parent with the end in mind.

What goals should we have for our children? Are they focused on making the ball team, getting into the right college, succeeding in business and finance, or marrying well? If those are our goals for our children, then we need to expand our horizons. Too many parents, whether they admit it or not, will seek to raise their children so that they (both parent and child) will achieve a desired social status. Some have parented in this way without consciously considering it, but let's not be shortsighted when it comes to eternity. Our goals in parenting should be centered on Christ and our child's relationship with Him.

So how do you parent with the goal of Christ in mind? Let me offer an illustration to help frame our thinking. My oldest son loves basketball. He spends hours playing basketball, working on drills, and working out to stay in shape. Let's imagine for a moment that his goal in life was to play in the NBA. Let's also imagine for a moment that my goal in life was to help my son achieve his goal.

If my parenting were focused on that singular goal, I would set out a plan, complete with milestones for certain age levels. We would work on hand-eye coordination at an early age. We would develop core strength to improve his quickness and speed. We would practice dribbling, shooting, and defense. We would make sure he understood offensive and defensive schemes. I would get him the appropriate instruction from coaches, feed him the correct diet, and get him into suitable competitive leagues. All of this would be based on a graduated scale so that he would improve with age, staying on the path for college ball and then the NBA.

It sounds like a good plan, doesn't it? The problem is that you haven't seen me and don't know that I am five feet, eight inches tall. I played football in high school, but my only natural athletic gift was that I could take a hit. My wife is lovely. She is beautiful, inside and out, but she doesn't bring much to the table in terms of basketball genes, either. If my son is going to make it to the NBA, he needs a miracle. He needs a genetic transplant to grow physically and to develop the skills necessary to play professional basketball. Apart from that miracle, it will not happen.

Parents, the same is true if your goal is for your child to have a relationship with Jesus. You can do all the right things to shape and mold them in the Christian faith. You can teach them the Word of God. You can raise them in a Bible-believing church. You can teach them morals and teach them to serve the poor. You can do all the right Christian things, but unless a miracle takes place, they will not grow to be followers of Christ. They don't need a gene transplant. They need a heart transplant. They must be born again.

That means when we parent with the end in mind, we pray with the end in mind. God is the one who changes hearts, so while we are shaping and molding their minds and their behaviors, we are praying like crazy for their hearts. As we spend time together in this book, we'll talk through what it means to shape our children and pray for them, ultimately trusting in the Father and His grace alone.

All this talk of shaping our children and parenting with the end in mind does have a danger to it that we need to address. It can make parenting seem like a formula. If we do x, then our children will turn out like y. We are not manufacturing children, and the temptation to do so will make us mechanical and rigid. Our children are not a product. They are our children. They are a gift from God and are meant to be enjoyed. Enjoy them. Delight in them as the Father delights in you.

Let me share another video story with you; this one is marked more by laughter than by beads of sweat and anger. My firstborn son once went on a date to the Sadie Hawkins dance at his school. This is the dance where the girls ask the boys, and his school takes this dance seriously. The kids dress in their finest, and "their finest" means a bow tie. My son doesn't know how to tie a bow tie, nor do I. But I love my son, and I wanted to help him out. There are videos for this sort of thing, so I watched several until I thought I was ready.

Armed with the basics, I stationed my son in front of the mirror. As I tried to tie his bow tie, my wife went to work with the video camera. Let's just put it this way: the video instructor said the tie should not look too perfect or people would think it was a clip-on. Well, there was no danger of that happening. My bow tie was awful, and now it was recorded for all to see. I turned to my wife and politely asked her to stop the camera.

We all laughed, and I remembered when this young man could fit in my two hands. There were some similarities between the two situations, but the contrasts were striking. I reflected on the work of God in our lives through tears and smiles, work and play, teaching and cutting up, and through it all, I could see that the Holy Spirit was using every single moment to shape us both.

In my parenting, I am learning the importance of intentionality. God calls me to be intentional with my kids in every little moment. This realization adds a certain weight to my time with my children. At the same time, it gives me peace to know that my impact on their lives is defined by the accumulation of moments rather than by any single snapshot.

A Thousand Pictures for a Thousand Moments

Have you ever seen a photo mosaic? A photo mosaic is a collection of thousands of small photographs all arranged to form one collective image. I believe the Lord has shown me that parenting is like that photo mosaic. Every moment with our children begins one of those thousands of tiny pictures. Each is important. Each is shaping them in some small way. Each requires intentionality. Yet, at the same time, each little picture comes together to form the collective image.

Our parenting—and our own growth spiritually—is shaped more by a thousand little moments over time than by any specific event we may experience or brilliant lesson we might hope to teach. We may be tempted to think that for our lives to *really* honor our God we must accomplish something extraordinary. But it's the ordinary, daily moments of parenting that reflect the good news of God's grace in Jesus. In the pages that follow I want to show you how to live and lead as a parent through those moments consistently over time, creating a mosaic that reflects the work of our loving God. We won't get it right every time, but over time the application of the gospel to every part of our children's lives will have the cumulative effect of forming a spiritual mosaic reflecting Jesus the way a gorgeous sunset displays God's creation.

I don't have to teach my children everything in one moment. Instead, I can enjoy them, delighting in them while I continue planting seeds. Isn't that what the Lord is doing in us? Isn't that Jesus's discipleship model—He took a group of fishermen, tax collectors, and zealots and spent intentional time with them, delighting in them and planting seeds for the kingdom? Yes, there were moments when He was frustrated with them. Yes, there were moments along the way when it was hard to see what the finished product might be. But Jesus didn't rush it. He was intentional. He prayed to the Father on their behalf and trusted that He would finish what He had begun.

Parent, He is doing the same in you, just as He is doing the same in me. So, let's spend some intentional time together in this book, allowing His Word to continue shaping us into parents who will love our children well for the glory of God. What do you say?

Section 1

The Foundation

Basics of Belief

Tryouts were coming soon, and our daughter Blair had set her goal of making the high school dance team. While dancing came naturally for Blair, this dance team performed with the marching band, which meant she would also be part of the flag team. She had danced almost since she could walk, but the flag was a new skill. She practiced. And practiced.

Blair spent hours tossing the flag in the air. In the beginning, she borrowed her brother's baseball helmet to protect herself, but eventually, she mastered the easy tosses. The easy tosses weren't the problem, however. The dreaded "45" loomed large on the horizon.

For those less versed in flag team maneuvers, the 45 is a flag team toss where the flag is thrown into what is more of an airborne spin than a vertical flip. This spin, however, is not supposed to be truly flat. The flag is meant to twirl through the air at a forty-five-degree angle, hence the name. As if that were not difficult enough, the girls aren't merely supposed to toss the flag into the air. They must catch it gracefully!

As you can imagine, such a toss does not come naturally. Instead, it requires hours of repetitive practice. Blair put in the practice, wearing scores of blisters on her hands. Then finally, the proud moment came when she landed her first 45. We jumped and cheered, but it was only one catch. She had to reach the point where she could land the 45 every time.

She had another issue driving her practice, however. You see, doing a 45 in the backyard is one thing. It is another to land it in the middle of a Friday night halftime routine while dancing, with the band playing all around you, with hundreds of people watching in the stands. She didn't have the time to think through every move. She had to develop muscle memory.

Muscle memory comes when your muscles know the mechanics without you consciously thinking about them. Blair had to train her muscles to do the same toss, with the same twirl and the same catch, all without thinking. It is the same for a basketball player shooting free throws. It is the same for a golfer hitting a tee shot. And believe it or not, it is the same for your parenting. The difference is that we are talking about something other than muscle memory with parenting. We are talking about heart memory.

As parents, and for that matter as human beings, we need to be so immersed in the truths of the gospel that they don't require conscious thought. We need to be so saturated with the gospel that we don't have to think about our relationship with the Father consciously. We need to be so saturated with the gospel that we don't have to think about our identity in Christ consciously. We need heart memory in the gospel. To come to this point in our Christian walk, we need the gospel massaged into every nook and cranny of our lives, moment after moment, which happens through daily repetition of the gospel . . . over a lifetime.

Why do you think this is so important for our parenting? If you are already a parent, say of teenagers, have you experienced their sudden emotional changes? Have you dealt with the dramatic, irrational questioning of their wardrobe, dinner selection, or family vacation spot?

Your reactions in those moments are probably a more accurate picture of your foundational beliefs than your reactions to those big situations you have time to prepare for. This is where heart memory comes in. We need heart memory in the gospel because our children need us to respond with

Jesus. We need heart memory because we need Jesus more than we need behavior tips.

So, we start with the foundational truths of God. These truths must undergird all the practical parenting discussions which will follow. Please resist the temptation you may be feeling to skip ahead to the practical application. You may have never heard these truths. If that is the case, soak in them. This may be the most life-changing material you will read.

Maybe, on the other hand, you long ago embraced the truths discussed in the following few chapters. If so, praise the Lord! Reread them. Be reminded. Be blessed and strengthen your heart's memory. And yet, others of us have heard these truths and wandered away from them. If this is you, please don't hear judgment or condemnation. Don't despair over what you haven't done. Read and hear the encouragement of Jesus Christ.

Over the following six chapters, we will begin (or continue) developing the heart memory we'll need throughout our parenting journey. We'll see the primacy of God's Word in all that we believe, say, and do. We'll be reminded of the beauty and fullness of the gospel. We'll look to the truth that our God is three persons in one God. We'll see how He relates to us through His covenant. We'll see how this truth of who God is and our place in Him affects the relationship between parent and child, reminding us who our children belong to. And finally, we'll look to God's design for the church and find hope in her role in our lives.

Are you ready? Let's train our hearts together.

CHAPTER 2

The Authoritative Word

God's Self-Revelation

All Scripture is breathed out by God and profitable for teaching, for reproof, for correction, and for training in righteousness, that the man of God may be complete, equipped for every good work.

—2 Timothy 3:16–17

Not too long ago, I had a question about my car audio system. I had been driving with my daughter, and she wanted to connect her phone to the car's Bluetooth so she could play her music. Before you read too much into it, this was a good thing. She's got great taste in music and has a much better selection than I do, so when she gets in the car, her choice takes precedence. The problem was I didn't know how to connect her phone, so I did what every American male does in similar situations. I started pushing buttons, sure I could figure it out on my own. Finally, after nothing worked, I heeded my daughter's advice, pulled the owner's manual out of the glove box, and looked it up. Once the problem was solved, I put the owner's manual back in the glove box. I haven't looked at it since.

How often do we treat the Bible the same way? We keep it in a familiar place, or at least we hope it's still there. When a problem comes up, we go pull it off the shelf, look in the concordance (the Bible version of a keyword index), and try to find a magic verse to apply to our situation/question/dilemma. After we have finished with the exercise, we put our Bible/owner's manual back up in its place so we can find it when we need it again.

Does any of this sound familiar? Maybe it describes your view of the Bible perfectly. Maybe it doesn't capture you completely, but you catch my drift. What's the problem with viewing the Bible the same way we view our car's owner's manual? For most of us, at least, the owner's manual is only used for reactionary purposes. We are reacting to some problem, so we go looking for a specific answer to a specific question without looking at the whole.

While the Bible does contain wisdom to aid our problem-solving/decision-making, it is so much more. The Bible is the very Word of God, and as such, it is the source of all truth. The Scriptures are not a reference manual that we merely go to in reactive mode. Instead, the Word of God is meant to be a shaping influence on our lives.

God's Self-Revelation

While in the fifth grade, each of my children had an opportunity to take a field trip to a nature camp in our state. We certainly don't live in an urban setting, but even small-town suburban kids are blessed with an opportunity to "return to nature." My wife and I alternated the chaperone duties, and we all enjoyed the adventure.

It was enjoyable being with the kids and getting to know their friends. During the day, we were exposed to all kinds of creatures, but at night the beauty of creation was fully displayed. One night during the trip, we took a night hike some distance away from the camp, far away from any man-made light. That was the whole point. Our guides took us out to the middle of nowhere. There, as we gazed up into the clear, night sky, we saw more stars than most of the kids had ever seen in their lives. It was beautiful and big. And in a good way, we felt small.

Psalm 19 opens in verse 1 by describing what we saw that night. "The heavens declare the glory of God, and the sky above proclaims his handiwork." As we stared up at the night sky, there was no doubt we were observing the creative beauty and power of our God. Romans 1:20 confirms that we were without excuse as to the knowledge of God. "For his invisible attributes, namely, his eternal power and divine nature, have been clearly perceived, ever since the creation of the world, in the things that have been made." And it didn't take that night in rural Alabama to see God's handiwork. All I needed to do was to investigate the faces of my children.

But what do we know about God by virtue of His creation? We know He is powerful. We know He is creative. We know He must be a God of order. These are good things to know, and in this knowledge, we can and will worship. But God knows we need more. He has given us His revealed Word, telling us more about Himself, about us, about sin, about redemption, about the Redeemer, about His plans for the church, for the family, for our lives, all of which are meant to bring Him glory.

The Authoritative Word

I've just described a big vision for the Bible and God's purpose for it in our lives. It is the foundation for all that Christians are to know and believe, the basis for all faith and practice. At this point, some of you may be saying, "Amen!" Others of you may be saying, "That's a tall order!" You might wonder who could be wise enough to capture *that* much truth. Put another way, *where* does the Bible come from?

That's not a new question, so the Bible takes an opportunity to address it. In 2 Peter 1:16–21, Peter deals with it, seemingly in response to those who wondered if the apostles were making up their stories. There, he begins by declaring himself to be an eyewitness to Jesus's transfiguration (see Matthew 17:1–3, Mark 9:2–8, and Luke 9:28–36) and an earwitness to God's audible declaration of Jesus as His beloved Son. In essence, he is saying, "I was there. I saw and I heard."

Wouldn't you like to have been there to have seen and heard as well? Many of us have said or thought that belief would have been so much easier if we could have walked in Jesus's presence. Peter seems to understand that thought, so he responds with an audacious statement. In verse 19 he goes on to say that "we have the prophetic word [the Scriptures] more fully confirmed ['more sure' in the NASB], to which you will do well to pay attention as to a lamp shining in a dark place, until the day dawns and the morning star rises in your hearts."

Peter is poetically describing the Scriptures as fixed. They do not change with our fading memory or our cloudy recollection of firsthand accounts. (They also don't change with our constantly changing cultural trends.) And he is urging us to pay attention because he didn't make them up. The Old Testament prophets didn't make them up. None of the human biblical writers made them up. They all wrote as they were carried along by the Holy Spirit (v. 21).

You and I can—and must—trust in the authoritative Word. Second Peter speaks of it as the inspired Word. Second Timothy 3:16 speaks of it as being "breathed out by God." This means you and I can trust in the authoritative Word in every area of life, especially in our parenting. The Bible is more than a resource guide to keep on the shelf. It is the foundation-shaping, worldview-forming source of all truth.[1]

The Sufficient Word

But what does *all truth* mean? How all-encompassing is *all*? Well, let me put it this way . . . the Scriptures are all the truth we need. Notice I didn't say all the facts or information you will use as you parent. You'll need to know practical life details about everything from family doctors, to school evaluations, to information about various sports and extracurricular activities, just to name a few. But these and many more pieces of information are inputs. We need inputs to parent, but without truth, we don't have a framework to analyze them.

---

[1] See Kevin DeYoung, *Taking God at His Word: Why the Bible Is Knowable, Necessary, and Enough, and What That Means for You and Me* (Wheaton, IL: Crossway, 2014). Some of you may want more on this subject. You may be wondering, "How do *you* know? Why is the Bible more true than fables or mythology?" Kevin DeYoung has written this helpful book to give you more confidence in the Word of God.

If you have not learned this yet, you soon will. Everyone has an opinion on parenting, whether they have ever been a parent or not. So how are we to navigate these waters? How are we to measure all the various nuggets of advice we receive? We must have a framework of truth. We need the Word. Let's allow the Word to shape our thinking and know that the shaping process will last a lifetime. Then, let's apply the Word that has shaped our thinking by thinking.

I add that last little admonition because we can be a lot like our kids. Often, one of my kids will ask me what they should do in a certain situation. Maybe it's in response to a friend who is inviting them to an event. Maybe they are trying to decide whether to participate in a certain activity. Maybe it's as simple as what should they wear (mind you, I don't often get that question).

I'll admit that when I get these types of questions, it is tempting to answer them. The problem is they are wanting me to make a decision that I am trying to equip them to make. When I give them a truth framework from which to decide, I want them to trust in the framework and in the rational mind God has given them, and then go decide. As parents, we need to do the same thing. Our Father is equipping us with the tool of His Word to make decisions as parents. Again, His Word is sufficient. Allow it to shape you and then think.

The Efficient Word

The Word is indeed sufficient as a foundation for faith and practice, for life and godliness. But is that all? Is it merely a tool to help us make better decisions? Absolutely not! Our primary need is not better thinking. Our primary need is for reconciliation with God, our Father, through Jesus Christ, who is revealed to us by the Holy Spirit. Our primary need and the primary need of our children is for salvation.

The Word is certainly sufficient to give us the knowledge of our sin and to point us to salvation in Jesus Christ. The apostle Paul makes this clear in many places but especially as he talks to Timothy, his child in the faith. In 2 Timothy 3:14–15, he encourages Timothy to continue in "the sacred writings [Scriptures], which are able to make you wise for salvation through faith in Christ Jesus."

"Able" certainly means that the Word is enough. But I believe it means more. "Able" also seems to point to the truth that the Scriptures are sufficient and *efficient* for salvation. There is power in the Word of God because it is not the word of man. It is, in fact, God's Word.

Elsewhere, Paul describes the Word's power as the power of God for salvation. In Romans 1:16, he says just this. The gospel, which means the good news of Jesus Christ, "is the power of God for salvation to everyone who believes." We need this efficient power source and so do our children.

There is a powerful and beautiful picture of the efficient Word in the book of Ezekiel. In chapter 37, the Spirit of the Lord led the prophet Ezekiel out into a valley. Many valleys provide a picturesque scene of the surrounding mountains; in contrast, another sight caught Ezekiel's attention. It was a scene of utter hopelessness in the valley of dry bones. Yet there, amid hopelessness, the Lord God commanded Ezekiel to speak the Word of God.

Though it seemed to make no rational sense, Ezekiel obeyed the command. He spoke the words God had given him: "O dry bones, hear the word of the LORD" (Ezekiel

37:4). There in the desperate valley of dry bones the sufficient Word was efficient to bring about life where only death had reigned. The Lord God raised the bones, bringing about new life. It was a miracle that points to the miracle of new birth required in the life of all who would call on the name of the Lord. This is the miracle of new birth brought about by the Spirit of God applying the Word of Christ to the hearts of the children of God.

As you lay a foundation of belief for your parenting, start here with the Word of God. If you are a new student of the Word, don't be intimidated by the text. The Bible is simple in what it teaches about salvation. At the same time, it is rich enough to fill a lifetime of soul-nourishing study. Also, don't be intimidated by those you deem as more advanced in the Word. Your kids don't need a seminary professor as a parent. They need a parent who is trusting and growing in the Word.

And for some of us, that truth is intimidating. Some of us don't read the Word, don't know where to start, and don't even know if we have a desire. It's OK. This describes most of us from time to time. It certainly explains much of my story. It describes struggles early on in my marriage when I struggled with spiritual leadership in my home. From time to time, it describes me as I can go through occasional seasons of dryness. If this is you, let me challenge you to pray a simple prayer. Pray that God the Father will give you a hunger and thirst for the Word. Pray this prayer and trust that the God who works through prayer will provide. And then feast on the Word, allowing it to shape you right where you are.

CHAPTER 3

A Gospel Primer

The Child Within Us

But when the fullness of time had come, God sent forth his Son, born of woman, born under the law, to redeem those who were under the law, so that we might receive adoption as sons.

—Galatians 4:4–5

Before learning to be parents, we must learn to be children. This is the very heart of the gospel. We are called to simple, childlike faith. Through God's grace, we're given the right to become children of God through childlike faith.

In churchy circles, we often speak of "the gospel," but do we know what it means? For those of us who have grown up around the culture of Christianity, there is a danger that this word *gospel* fades into the background of familiarity. We're comfortable with its presence but unclear as to its purpose.

21

When this happens, we miss the fullness of the Christian life, and our parenting misses the power of grace.

The gospel must inform our parenting, but before that can happen, our hearts must be versed in it. At the core, *the gospel* refers to the good news that Jesus came to save sinners who have been separated from God because of their sin. Through Christ's finished and gracious work on behalf of God's elect, those sinners are reconciled back to the Father, not because they were worthy of it but because Jesus was worthy. Jesus willingly made this sacrifice out of His great love for those whom the Father has given Him.

Maybe that is a new thought for some of us. Perhaps we haven't thought of the gospel in terms of reconciliation. To *reconcile* means to bring back together. For that to happen, God had to do certain things in us, and we need to spend time understanding what those things were and are. We do so not to be well versed in the mechanics of redemption but to fall more deeply in love with God. By doing this, we can point our children to a personal relationship with Christ that is marked by deep love.

Some of us grew up with an idea that the Christian faith is about what we do and don't do. Yet, the heart of the gospel is not about moralism. It is about a relationship. That relationship is based not on what we do but on what Jesus has done. What He has done has been to call us to a relationship that the New Testament describes in terms of our adoption into the family of God.

Regeneration: Not a Better You—An Entirely New You[2]

When our first child was born, Anna and I believed a true miracle had happened. I'm not talking about the miracle of birth. I'm talking about something more profound. We believed that Anna had just given birth to the first lovely baby. I mean, newborn babies are often cute but not beautiful. We had seen the videos in our prenatal classes. Newborn babies look more like lizards than humans. But not our son. He was perfect.

Well, at least that is the way we saw him for a few moments. I've already shared the story of his first bath, but the saga continued. While we still believe him to be a handsome young man, the truth has set in. We've learned that though he was a beautiful baby, there were far deeper issues underneath his angelic appearance. Deep down, he was more like that lizard in the first place. Or maybe a close cousin to the lizard, a snake.

There is something we must know about our children and ourselves. We were born with a cobra heart. That's right; we were born with a fatal heart condition impacting our entire being. Sometimes we call it our nature. We don't need a degree in Latin to understand the name of this disease. It is called sin.

Over the years, I've taught my children to do a lot of things. I've taught them to throw a football. I've tried to teach

---

[2] Much of this gospel framework has been shaped by Dr. Henry Krabbendam. Dr. Krabbendam is a mentor of mine who has taught me much about what he calls the threefold gospel: your three problems and God's three solutions.

them to eat well. I've taught them to tie shoes, swim, and ride bicycles. But I never had to teach them to talk back to authority. I never had to teach them to hit, steal, or lie. That is because they were born with the same diseased heart that I was born with. And all of that hitting, stealing, and lying was my children acting out of their true nature.

What does a cobra do? A cobra kills its prey. That's its nature. If you were to encounter a cobra, I wouldn't advise trying to train it. Instead, the cobra needs to be killed. The same is true of our sinful nature. We aren't sinners because we sin. We sin because we are sinners, which means instead of cleaning up our act, we need a new nature.

We're talking about the need for regeneration. The Bible calls this the *new birth*. God promised it in Ezekiel 36:26. Jesus spoke of it in John 3:3 when He was questioned by Nicodemus. There, Jesus told Nicodemus that his heart condition had rendered him blind. Nicodemus was blind to his true nature and the identity of Jesus. Before he could respond in faith, he needed the blinders removed from his heart. He needed to be born again.

You don't change your nature. It is who you are, so for that to change, something external must happen. The Holy Spirit must "remove the heart of stone" and "give you a heart of flesh" (Ezekiel 36:26). Paul wrote of this in 2 Corinthians 5:17 when he said, "Therefore, if anyone is in Christ, he is a new creation. The old has passed away; behold, the new has come." This was the true miracle that my child needed.

That need for a miracle in our own lives and in the lives of our children gives us a beautiful new appreciation for the work of Christ on our behalf. That the Lord had to radically change our entire nature tells us the desperate measures the

Lord has taken to save us. That must inform our parenting. As we begin to see the reality of our precious children's true sin natures, it helps us understand their need, not for behavior modification but for Christ. That realization must drive us to prayer for only the Spirit of God can bring about the work of new life in our children.

Justification: Guilt Removed, Righteousness Given

If someone were to ask us what happened on the cross, we might say something like "Jesus died for my sins." For many years that was my answer. It is a true answer. The problem is that it is only a half-truth, and in the half-truth, we miss out on the joy and freedom of the Christian life. What is the other half? Jesus gave us His righteousness.

In 2 Corinthians 5:21 we read, "For our sake he made him to be sin who knew no sin, so that in him we might become the righteousness of God." This verse describes the glorious transaction which took place on the cross. Jesus, who knew no sin, became sin, taking all our sin upon himself. I describe it as glorious because what we received in exchange was His righteousness.

Have you ever heard of The Color Run? It is a five-kilometer road race where the participants are doused in paint as they run. That may not sound like your kind of fun (mine either), but my wife and daughter loved it. They started the race clean, wearing white T-shirts. Along the way, though, race volunteers threw buckets of paint over them.

The race promoters describe it as the "Happiest 5K on the Planet." That would certainly match with the group photos I saw afterward. The girls looked like smiling rainbows overdue for baths. It was great fun, but the whole picture points me to a less-fun image.

On the cross, Jesus was covered not in rainbow-colored paint but in our sin. I imagine a different facial expression. On the cross, Jesus's face must have grimaced as every bit of our sin—past, present, and future—was thrown on Him. The perfect one was made to be sin for us. This is what it means for our guilt to be taken. It was thrown on Jesus, who bore the full wrath of God on the cross for all the sins of God's children for all time. There on the cross our legal guilt was removed! As incredible as this sounds, it was only half of what happened. Jesus took our sin and, in exchange, gave us His perfect righteousness.

Throughout the years, my kids have participated in various activities, sports, and dances. Some of those required tryouts to make the teams. When they made the team, they got the jersey. They were on the team. For one year. Then the process started all over again.

That meant they could enjoy the successful tryout for about one night. Then they had to get up the next morning and start working again, improving their skills, because they'd have to try out again the next year.

In Christ Jesus the opposite happens. We don't have to worry about repeat tryouts. We are His permanently, clothed in Christ's righteousness. That way, when God the Father looks down on us, He sees the righteousness of Jesus.

Many of us have been told we don't have to perform for God. But have we fully embraced this reality? How would it feel to know that because of Jesus's sacrifice for us, we never have to try out again? We can breathe deeply knowing that

His love for us and that our place in the family are secure because of what Jesus has done on our behalf. We can rest knowing that it is all His grace and is received through faith alone, in Christ alone.

Theologians from Paul's day to ours call this justification by faith. The person on the street calls it resting in Christ. As parents, we need to know it as the basis of our identity in Christ. Our identity doesn't depend on whether our children pitch a fit in the restaurant. It doesn't depend on our children's grades. It doesn't depend on anything related to our children. Instead, it depends on whether we are children of God through faith in Christ.

How might it impact our parenting if we truly knew Christ as the foundation of our identity? How might it change our motivations in raising our children if we weren't training them like circus animals to do tricks for others but instead were pointing them to the same life-giving relationship with the Savior that we enjoy?

It changes everything! In the moment we may forget and turn to anger or despair. But in those moments, we must go back to God's Word to be reminded of precious gospel truths. We must go back to continue training our hearts and forming the heart memory we've talked about. And then we can continue breathing deeply in the justifying love of Christ.

Sanctification: You Are, So Be

For some of us these beautiful truths of the gospel are a refreshing reminder. For some this is radical news. For most of us something inside resists because we think it's too good to be true. Maybe the idea of justifying grace is so diametrically opposed to the message we hear in all of life that we can't accept it.

We live in a world that seems to be built upon an endless stream of "if-then" propositions. *If* we study hard, *then* we will make good grades. *If* we go to the right school, *then* we will get a good job. *If* we are beautiful, smart, and athletic, *then* we will be worthy of a desirable spouse. *If* we eat our vegetables, *then* we will be healthy and can go outside to play. Our lives are impacted by this "if-then" mindset in innumerable ways.

Set against this message, the gospel of Jesus Christ says no to "if-then" thinking and gives us another form of logic: "you are, so be." In Christ, *you are* righteous, *so be* who He has already declared you to be. In Christ, *you are* a beloved child of God, *so be* a child of God. In Christ *you are* redeemed, *so be* who you are in Him.

Some of us look at the huge gap that exists between the righteousness of Christ and the everyday reality of our thought lives, our actions, our parenting, our desires, and we want to throw up our hands in despair. If this is you, let me encourage you with the words of Philippians 1:6. "And I am sure of this, that he who began a good work in you will bring it to completion at the day of Jesus Christ."

Paul is saying it's OK. God is not finished with us. Don't lose heart. The story of redemption that God has written in creation and our lives is just that, a story. We are somewhere in the middle of the book. But this story is written in ink. The end is certain. Elsewhere, Paul writes in Romans 8:30, "And those whom he predestined he also called, and those whom he called he also justified, and those whom he justified, he also glorified." Our story is written with a gloriously happy ending, and that ending is so certain, Paul wrote of our glorification in the past tense.

But what about the daily struggles of growth in this life? I believe it is the same for us in our parenting as it is for the people of the church where I pastor. When I describe our church, I describe us as a people who *have been* transformed by the grace of the Lord Jesus Christ and who *are being* transformed by the grace of the Lord Jesus Christ.

I believe that is what Hebrews 10:14 points out. "For by a single offering he has perfected for all time those who are being sanctified." Jesus has transformed us. He has made us holy. Jesus is still transforming us. He is making us holy.

Parents, we need to know this truth in our own lives. If we are in Christ, our status is secure, but we are still works in progress. Our lives as Christians are marked by growth in grace, but we don't have preset goals that God expects us to meet at certain points along the way. He is not looking at us with a disappointed scowl on His face, wishing we could do better. When He looks upon us, He sees the righteousness of Christ. And through Christ, we are now adopted children of the King! Adoption is the context of the Christian life. We grow, but as we grow, we remain beloved children of a good, good Father.

While this is true of us as parents, it is also the framework for our parenting. Our greatest goal is to point our children to a relationship with Jesus Christ, so our parenting should be informed by the way our Father parents us.

Recently I was at the baseball complex in our town. I've been there quite a bit over the years and have seen the same scene played out countless times. A competitive parent yelled at his son in disapproval. It was a shaming act telling the boy that he had better shape up if he wanted to be accepted by his team or by his family. The boy walked onto the field dejected. His shoulders slumped over. A couple of the boys walked over to him and put an arm around his shoulders, but the damage was done.

The boy had heard from his father, "If you play well, then you will be accepted." The gospel tells us, "You are my beloved son, so simply be my son." Yes, there is still growth to be had. Yes, there is still discipline to be dispensed. Yes, there is still shaping that will take place, but the difference is one of security in our status.

This gospel truth is also meant for parents. If we are in Christ, our status is secure in the family of God, not because of our proficiency in parenting but because of the eternal love of God and the finished work of Christ.

CHAPTER 4

The Triune God

Majesty and Mystery

---

*The grace of the Lord Jesus Christ and the love of
God and the fellowship of the Holy Spirit be with
you all.*

—2 Corinthians 13:14

If our vision of parenting is to point our children to a life-altering relationship with God, then we must have some sense of who He is. More importantly, if we are to navigate the often murky and exhausting waters of parenting, then we need more than a sense of who He is. We need a relationship with God. To live in a relationship with our children, we must know them, and we must continue growing in our knowledge of them. This is certainly true of our relationship with God as well. We began our exploration of foundational beliefs with a gospel primer, helping us understand our place as children of God. Let us continue by exploring the majestic and mysterious biblical truth that our God exists as three persons and one God.

For many of us who have grown up in the church, our exposure to the Trinity was reduced to some illustration regarding the three phases of water or the connection between an eggshell, an egg white, and an egg yolk. The Trinity was a mental puzzle we tried to solve through illustration.

For those of us who grew up with the catechisms of the church, we memorized the sixth question to the Westminster Shorter Catechism: "There are three persons in the Godhead: The Father, the Son, and the Holy Spirit; and these three are one God, the same in substance, equal in power and glory."[3] While this is a very meaty (and brief) statement on the Trinity, it hardly engages the heart. Maybe it is no wonder we pause at the thought of a book on parenting including a whole chapter on the Trinity. Parenting is the most challenging and life-giving work we will ever do. To flourish, we'll need more than a superficial knowledge of God.

Consider the difference between looking at a picture of an airplane and riding in the copilot's seat. I suppose a two-dimensional image we see on a page can tell us something about the airplane. Maybe if we have good imaginations, we can picture ourselves flying in it. But for a moment, contrast the experience of viewing a two-dimensional image on a page with the thrill of sitting in the cockpit during flight. Looking

---

[3] Catechisms are theological summaries communicated through a series of questions and answers. The Westminster Shorter Catechism accompanies the Westminster Confession of Faith and the Westminster Larger Catechism. Many reformed churches use these catechisms for instructional purposes.

through the cockpit window, feeling the speed, the turns, the shifts in elevation would give us an entirely new perspective.

With the experience of real live flight, the mere two-dimensional image will never again satisfy. We don't focus on the Triune God to win points in a Bible trivia contest. Mere comprehension is not our purpose. No, our goal is to experience the beauty of God's fullness that we might rest our parenting in him. A full trinitarian view of God explodes our small view of the gospel and provides a rich texture for our gospel parenting.

As we speak of the Trinity, we'll spend a few moments exploring the roles of the three persons within the Trinity. However, before we look to the persons of the Trinity individually, we need to set an umbrella of understanding. An umbrella covers everything that lies beneath its protective shade. This umbrella I speak of is formed by the love and understanding within the intra-trinitarian relationship. When we speak of the Trinity, we need to see that the individual roles of the three members of the Trinity all find meaning in terms of their eternal relationship.

As parents (and as believers in this world), the first thing we need to see about the Trinity is that the Father, Son, and Holy Spirit have existed for all eternity in a mutually loving union which Jesus describes in terms of oneness. In John 17, Jesus prays for the disciples and for us. In His prayer, He prays that believers would be one, just as the Father is in Him and He is in the Father (John 17:21). During His prayer, He goes on to describe the love which has existed for all eternity within their union (John 17:23–24).

Why, though, is this specifically important for parents? There are a host of reasons, but they all relate to the fact that God is love and loving, and His love predates us. Think about it. Your children need to know their parents love one another. The love their parents have for one another teaches them much about love and relationships, and the love the parents have for their children is a derivative of the love they have for one another.

For some, this discussion of the love parents have for one another may come with a sting. Some of us are in loveless marriages, while some of us are single parents. While we may feel a sting with this discussion, we probably also understand it on a level too deep for words.

Be encouraged. God the Father, God the Son, and God the Holy Spirit have existed for all eternity in an eternally loving union. God's love for His children is a derivative of the love He has within the Trinity. As His children, regardless of the state of our marriages, or whether we are even in a marriage, we can take comfort in his love.

The next thing I would say in terms of an umbrella of understanding is that within this eternally loving union, the members of the Trinity have specific roles in the context of their relationship. We see some of this explained in 1 Corinthians 11:3 and are told there of the implications of this separation of roles in our relationships. There Paul writes, "But I want you to understand that the head of every man is Christ, the head of a wife is her husband, and the head of Christ is God."

God the Father is the head of God the Son, and within this framework of headship, God the Father and God the Son exist in loving union. God the Spirit proceeds from the Father and Son yet exists in this same eternally loving union. This love and these roles help us grow in love and understanding of our roles within the family. This love and these roles also help give context to our understanding of the persons within the Trinity.

The Father — Sovereign God

One of the scariest moments I've had in parenting, or maybe I should say the first scary moment I had, was when Anna and I left the hospital with our firstborn. We were leaving the hospital with a human being who was utterly dependent upon us for survival, and we had no idea what we were doing. It was the loneliest moment of our young lives.

The doctors and nurses in the hospital had been there to help with all our questions, and now it felt like they were sending us out into the cold, cruel world to figure things out all on our own. I still remember thinking, "I sure hope we get this right."

Many of us have experienced fear, thinking fixing our problems was up to us. We're not alone if we've ever thought this. But there is another sense in which we are not alone. We are not alone because God is at work in His creation, and the Father's work is always perfect.

Yet we forget, and that is where the fear enters in. We'll speak more about this sinister attack on our parenting later, but we need to also address it as we consider the Trinity. The opportunities for fear abound. Those fears can have the effect of locking parents up like a car that won't shift into drive. We don't know which direction to turn, so we don't turn at all. Fortunately, Jesus has some things to say about fear. In Matthew 10:29–31, He tells us two sparrows are sold for a penny, meaning they are of very little monetary value, yet not one of them falls to the ground apart from the Father. At the same time, every hair on our head and our children's heads are numbered. Jesus tells us this to combat fear, reminding us that we are of far greater value than the sparrows.

The implication is this: the Father who created us and our children knows us and cares for us. As parents, we would like to take the next step in this argument and take it to mean that our children will never hurt. Yet, that is not the Father's promise. His promise is that He knows them and loves them. He is sovereign over creation. We can be freed from the fear that locks up our decision-making for our children.[4]

On the other hand, not all our fears for our children are related to bumps and bruises. Our deeper fears are often centered on their faith in Christ. To combat these fears, the truth of the Father is also a great comfort. The Father loves His children with an eternal, electing love.

> Blessed be the God and Father of our Lord Jesus Christ, who has blessed us in Christ with every spiritual blessing in the heavenly places, even as he chose us in him before the foundation of the world, that we should be holy and blameless before him. In love he predestined us for adoption to himself as sons through Jesus Christ, according to the purpose of his

---

[4] See Kevin DeYoung, *Just Do Something: A Liberating Approach to Finding God's Will* (Chicago: Moody, 2009). For some of us this fear around decision-making is connected to a misunderstanding of how to understand God's will and whether we are in it. Though DeYoung is not specifically speaking to parents in this book, he very helpfully (and simply) guides us in understanding what it means to be "in God's will."

will, to the praise of his glorious grace, with which he has blessed us in the Beloved. (Ephesians 1:3–6)

The Father has loved His children with a "grace before time" kind of love. He loves our children more than we do. This does not mean that we are passive when it comes to the gospel faith of our children, but it does mean that we are not alone. As we parent our children, we trust in our powerful and loving Father. And we are called to raise our children to know this Father.

There is one more aspect of the Father's love that we parents need to be reminded of. As we parent, we are not working *for* the Father's approval. We are working *from* the Father's approval. If you are in Christ, you are His. You are already accepted. There is nothing more to prove!

The Son—Incarnate God

One of my favorite verses in all of Scripture is John 1:14. "And the Word became flesh and dwelt among us, and we have seen his glory, glory as of the only Son from the Father, full of grace and truth." I love this verse because it speaks to my deep need of Jesus and of His profound response: He came to me.

When our children were little, they responded in different ways on the nights when they couldn't sleep. If the boys were up, they came running to our bedroom. *Sometimes* they were demanding something. *Always* they came to tell me what they needed.

Our daughter was different. If she couldn't sleep, she either crawled or walked to the hallway outside her bedroom. And there she stayed. She would lie there on the floor and cry. You see when Blair was hurting, she needed Daddy to come to her where she was. It was her form of saying, "Come to me. Come where I am, where I am hurting."

How about us? Isn't there something that is more comforting about help coming to us, rather than having to go out and find it? We parents are the same. We need help. We need comfort. And our Savior has come to us to dwell with us. In doing so, He has revealed something of God's glory to us. He has revealed the depths of His love. He has also revealed the depth of His humility.

As parents, we can take comfort in the truth of Jesus, our incarnate God, who came to us to experience our trials, to love us in our mess, and to secure our salvation. As parents, we can take comfort in the truth that Jesus came to our children for the same reasons. Finally, as parents, we can learn from Jesus in the way He comes.

We've already spoken of the primacy of the gospel, both for our lives as parents and our task of parenting. Those gospel truths were secured by a person, Jesus Christ. As we grow in knowing Him, we can take comfort in knowing our children share in the same hope that gives us peace. Jesus is the Savior who has come to save sinners like our children. We can take heart. In the moments of ugly disobedience, we can remember that Jesus has come. He didn't run from sin, not even ours. Instead, He came and took that sin on Himself.

Also know that while Jesus is not primarily a role model, we can take cues from His ministry. We'll talk more about this when we speak of discipling our children, but for now, I am focused on the fact that His ministry was incarnational, meaning He did not remain distant but instead entered our world. Jesus came to us in our mess. For us this means we go to our children to love them and minister to them in their messiness. Our parenting is not meant to be kept at arm's length. Jesus, the head of the church, has modeled this for us.

More than a role model, though, Jesus is the one who secured salvation. There have been times when we have messed up in our Christian walk, yet our relationship with Christ is secure because of Him, not us. There will be times when we'll mess up in leading our children in their Christian walks. In those moments, we can find comfort in knowing their relationship with Christ is ultimately dependent upon Christ and not upon our cunning.

When we consider the sovereignty of God the Father, there can be a temptation to think of Him as a cold and distant God. Resist this temptation. Our sovereign and electing Father sent Jesus to secure our salvation on the cross. He came to us!

The Holy Spirit—Indwelling God

Many of us parents remember that lonely feeling when we left the hospital with our firstborn. Many of us were wishing we could take the nurses home to teach us all the things that we didn't even know we didn't know. I imagine the disciples might have had similar feelings. In Matthew 28, Jesus gave them some last-minute instructions before He went to be with the Father. Those last-minute instructions are what we call the Great Commission. Jesus was leaving, but He told the disciples to go preach the gospel and build the church. I would imagine they had a certain sense of loneliness as well!

But as Jesus was instructing them (and us), He included a beautiful promise. "Behold, I am with you always, to the end of the age" (Matthew 28:20). Jesus was telling the disciples they were not alone in their mission. He was giving them a glorious and rewarding job, but He promised He would be the power source. It was a promise He fulfilled at Pentecost when He sent the Holy Spirit.

The same comfort the disciples must have felt at the presence of the Holy Spirit is also meant to comfort us as parents. Maybe we haven't thought about these terms. Maybe we haven't considered the ministry of the Holy Spirit in our parenting. If not, we can find encouragement. All that the Father has decreed and all that the Son has secured is applied in the lives of individuals by the indwelling presence of the Holy Spirit.

Have you ever wondered if your children would ever grow in maturity? Have you ever wondered if the gospel lessons and life lessons you have tried to teach would ever sink in? Many of us have lost sleep over these questions and over the struggle for Christian growth in our own lives. We can rest from our worry over our missed teaching moments, knowing that the Spirit of God is at work in the lives of our children just like He is at work in our lives.

Do you remember how we talked about the photo mosaic? The photo mosaic is a collection of hundreds of tiny photographs which come together to form one beautiful image. We talked about this being a picture of our parenting. It is an encouraging thought, but we struggle with it. We think we've got to come up with the right saying or the right rule so that our children magically turn into perfectly obedient boys and girls. But it doesn't happen that way because it doesn't happen that way in us either.

We plant seeds in our children's lives, and then we trust in the Lord for growth. The Holy Spirit is the member of the Godhead working that growth in their lives. And He is *always* with them. In many ways, our parenting is a daily work of partnering with the Holy Spirit to shape the hearts of our children. This reality should encourage us and should drive us to prayer.

This truth about our Triune God is intensely practical for our parenting. If we sincerely believed that God really is sovereign, that belief would certainly impact our worrying. Rather than losing sleep, weight, and hair over the health, happiness, and spiritual well-being of our children, we might pray more.

Galatians 2:20 is true when it tells us the reason Jesus went to the cross to die was that He loved us and our children. If we genuinely believed this truth, it would impact the gap which exists between what we profess to believe and the actual places we go for love and affirmation. It would also impact the places we send our children for love and affirmation, places like Little League sports, dance, or report cards. To be loved like this must affect us and our parenting!

What if the Holy Spirit really does dwell in our children and us? God's Word is true in John 14:15–17 where Jesus tells us He will not leave us as orphans but will send another Helper, the Holy Spirit, who will dwell in us. If we truly believed we have the power of God dwelling inside of us, it would change our prayer lives. If we practically believed the Spirit of God would guide us in the Word, it would fuel our desire to read the Word and to teach it to our children.

The doctrine of the Trinity may not come to mind when we are trying to figure out the right bedtime schedule for

41

our children, but it has a profound effect on our parenting. Know that as we are building a foundation of belief for our parenting. The truth of our Triune God will bless our souls, and it will bless the way we care for the souls of our children.

CHAPTER 5

The Covenant-Making God

Promise as Premise

For this is the covenant that I will make with the house of Israel after those days, declares the LORD: I will put my law within them, and I will write it on their hearts. And I will be their God, and they shall be my people.

—Jeremiah 31:33

My friend has a unique way of making the profound simple. We were talking about God's covenant promise as it related to his children and his parenting, and that's when he said it. "I'm more confident in God's promise than I am in the thought I'll be some jam-up father."

If you are not from Alabama, let me translate something for you. *Jam-up*, at least as my friend was using it, means to be highly proficient and effective. My friend was not shirking his responsibilities as a father. He understood and eloquently communicated that his hopes for his children's well-being, namely their salvation in Christ, were dependent upon God's work in their lives. He also understood and communicated that this was not blind hope. He was hoping for a promise that God had made. So, what is this promise?

God's Vision Statement

Another friend of mine once told me he believed God's vision statement was captured in Jeremiah 31:33: "I will be their God, and they shall be my people." We were talking about vision and mission statements for our church, and my friend was using this statement as an illustration of how God might summarize His vision for His people.

It is an interesting and profound statement. It is also a thought, which when traced, takes us on an extensive journey through Scripture. Reference Bibles are helpful tools for our study of Scripture as they show the connections between various texts. It is an encouraging exercise to trace the references pointed out in Jeremiah 31:33. When we do this, following the thread by tracing the referenced verses, we see this promise stretching back to the beginning of Scripture and extending forward all the way to the new heavens and new earth.

This journey through the Bible shows us that God made this promise to Abraham and his offspring after him in Genesis 17:7–8. He confirmed and clarified it for the nation of Israel in Exodus 6:7 and Leviticus 26:12. The promise was a central theme of the prophets as they brought God's Word to the nations of Israel and Judah leading up to, in the midst of, and upon return from exile (Isaiah 59:21; Jeremiah 30:22; 31:33; 32:38; Ezekiel 36:28; Hosea 2:23; Zechariah 8:8; 13:9).

In the church age of the New Testament, God's Word tells us this promise continues in and through the church (Acts 2:39; Hebrews 11:16; 1 Peter 2:9–10). Then finally, we see the glorious fulfillment of the promise in Revelation 21:3 and 7 as the Lord God takes up residence among His people in the new heavens and new earth.

This little snapshot merely scratches the surface, but it illustrates the truth that God's covenant promise and its fulfillment is the central theme of Scripture. God, of His own volition, has chosen to love an unlovely people and by His grace to make them His own. He has promised this glorious vision, and through the story line of scripture, we see that He keeps His promise.

Now, let's try to personalize this a bit. God states this promise beautifully by telling us that we are *His* people. But what does that mean? It means He claims us as His own and that we belong to Him!

At this point, let me offer another translation. I translated my Alabama friend's lingo. Let me translate my Georgia lingo. When I'm back home, I'll speak of *my* people. When I say, "These are my people," I mean it endearingly and so does God! He is claiming us as His people!

My children seem to understand this intuitively. They love their extended family. They love grandparents. They love cousins. And they love to be claimed by their family, extended or otherwise. While it is not the primary point I am trying to make with this discussion of God's covenant, it's important, nonetheless. Let's claim our children—privately and publicly—in the good times and in the bad. Don't just claim them when they win the race. Claim them when they fall, and even when they misbehave. Let them know that they are "our people" and that this is the way we are claimed by the Lord our God!

Accomplishing the Vision Through Families

God's covenant promises to be God to His people and to claim His people as His own are indeed beautiful. The basis my friend had in trusting in that promise for his daughter was that he trusted in God's Word.

In Genesis 17:7–8, God's promise to Abraham was also a promise to (and through) Abraham's offspring. This promise to bless and work through families was reiterated in Acts 2:39. In some sense, God seems to be saying that the promise of grace, which is received by faith, is also a promise to the children of believers.

Upon hearing this biblical truth, some of us may be tempted to think to ourselves: "Great! It sounds like our kids are a sure thing!" It may be tempting to think this way, but what do we mean by *sure thing*? Are we simply chalking up this promise as an indicator of whether our children will get into heaven?

First, let's think differently about our children's salvation than in terms of getting into heaven. Their salvation implies a real, present relationship with Jesus. Secondly, when we speak of God accomplishing His vision through families, we are not speaking of automatic acceptance. Let's look at the idea of the covenant to dig a little deeper.

Trust in the Promise

A covenant is an agreement, like a legal document. It describes the obligations of both parties and lays out the blessings and curses which will accompany those obligations. God's covenant with man is gracious. He initiated it. He said what He would do. He declared that He would be our God and we would be His people. It was a promise, or a covenant, made with Abraham and repeated throughout scripture to Abraham's (spiritual) offspring.

In Genesis 17:7, Isaiah 59:21, and Acts 2:39, this promise is made to those who believe in God's plan of redemption through Jesus and to their children. While we don't parent with a sure-thing mentality, as Christian parents, we do have the gift of presumption. We trust in the promise of God, so we presume that He is working in their hearts, wooing them to Himself.

I once had a conversation with a young man who wrestled with some of these questions. He was one of four children in a Christian family. Both of his parents were believers, yet one of his siblings had abandoned the faith. This sibling's abandonment had been difficult for the parents, but my young friend was trying to work through it in his own way. He asked me, as a parent, if we should just expect some of our kids not to follow Christ. By his way of thinking, three kids out of four following Jesus seemed like pretty good results.

My young friend was trying to work through how he might approach parenting when the time came for him to raise children to know Christ. His approach, however, was fatalistic and heartbreaking. "No!" I cried out to him. "I would never settle for three out of four as if I were determining a batting average." I was trying to explain to my young friend that in parenting, we don't play the odds. We trust in the promise.

That was preparatory training for my young friend. For some of us, it is an oftentimes painful reality. Some of us are dealing with the pain of children who seem to be abandoning Christ. It's important for us to affirm the pain of experiencing our children seemingly turning away from Christ. We'll speak more to this later in the book. For now, though, let's reiterate that God's promise of a Redeemer, fulfilled in Jesus Christ, is always the source of our hope. Christ is the only hope for the believer. Christ is the only hope for the not-yet believer. As we parent in the light of God's covenant, we trust in His promise, but we also rest in mystery.

Rest in the Mystery

Some of us (like me) are logical. We like things to make sense. We want a plan and believe if we follow that plan to its conclusion, we'll be able to predict the outcome. The problem is when we try to condense God's wisdom to a plan we can understand and then work to control the outcome, we make ourselves out to be God.

This is where the truth of our covenant-making God begins to mess with our logical minds. There are two truths we find in Scripture. One is that God is sovereign over His creation. He is sovereign over our lives and over the lives of our children. He has ordained the end from the beginning, working all things in history for His glory, pointing to the eventual fulfillment of His kingdom in the new heavens and new earth. We read this truth everywhere in scripture.

But there is a second truth we find in scripture that is equally clear. Humans are responsible for their own actions and will be judged accordingly. While God is sovereign over all that we do and over all that will be done to us and our families, we are also responsible for the decisions we make regarding our families.

These two truths don't fit neatly into our desire for a logically ordered plan. We can't understand how they fit together. Some of us have wrestled between what we've considered two opposing positions. We tend to lean in one direction or another until we began to see that God's wisdom and His ways are not like ours. Isaiah 55:8–9 states it so clearly.

> For my thoughts are not your thoughts,
> neither are your ways my ways, declares the LORD.
> For as the heavens are higher than the earth,
> so are my ways higher than your ways
> and my thoughts than your thoughts.

God is God, and we are not, which means that through Jesus, we have the freedom to worship Him as God and to rest in the mystery that is His wisdom.

Others of us don't have a problem acknowledging that God's ways are mysterious, but we still want to know how God works through families. We want a clear and intellectually satisfying answer. The problem is that it is a mystery. Throughout Scripture, we read that the promise is for you and for your offspring after you. We see Him working through families, calling children to Himself. Throughout Scripture, we also see children turn from the Lord.

With what we view as conflicting evidence, we wonder if God's covenant promises to work through families are still in effect. We wonder what it means for our children and for our parenting. Yes, God's covenant promise to bless the offspring of believers is timeless. It means that in a special, mysterious way, our children are holy to the Lord. We trust in His promise while resting in the mystery, all along pointing them to Jesus.

Point to Jesus

At the risk of revealing way too much of my sinful idolatry, I'll share with you one of the bedtime routines I enjoyed with my young children. I sang to them. Apparently, at that point in their development they had not yet acquired musical ears, so they would rest in my arms and listen.

Almost without fail, I sang three songs to them each night: "Jesus Loves Me," "Amazing Grace," and my college alma mater's fight song. Why those three songs? Well, I knew the words for one thing. But I was also letting them know what was important to our family. Call it brainwashing (in the case of the fight song) or call it nurturing their hearts (in the case of "Jesus Loves Me" and "Amazing Grace"). I was pouring into them early on, trying to shape them.

God's covenant promises to work through our families do not mean that we leave our children to themselves to learn of the gospel of Jesus Christ. On the contrary, we trust in God's promise and point our children to the Savior. By growing up in Christian homes under the loving care of Bible-believing churches, our children have the blessing of participation in the covenant community. But their relationship with Jesus will ultimately be a personal matter.

Romans chapter 3 speaks to this. In Romans 3:1, Paul asks the question that is on the minds of his readers, "Then what advantage has the Jew?" In context, he speaks of their circumcision, which prior to baptism, was the old covenant sign of their participation in the covenant community (that is, the church in the new covenant). In verse 2, he answers his question by saying there are many advantages. They have the Word of God.

However, later in verse 9 Paul almost seems to contradict himself, acknowledging that for the Jews their advantage does not leave them better off. While they had the Word of God, they still were sinners. The same is true for us. We have an advantage by virtue of our membership in a Christian family and a Christian church, but our sins must be dealt with. We must turn to the Lord Jesus Christ in faith and repentance. The same is true for our children.

We know this truth, but we can also neglect its implications. On one of my trips to Uganda, I walked the streets of Lira sharing the gospel. I came upon a young teenager and asked him if I could talk to him about Jesus. He replied that he was a Christian. Delighted at the response, I asked if he would share his testimony with me. He told me his mother was a Christian, and he had been to church with her a few times. That was it. He knew nothing of his sin and the cross of Christ. Essentially, he had adopted the cultural label of *Christian* because that was how his mother identified herself.

I asked this young man if I could tell him more. We walked through scripture where I pointed out his need for a new heart, for the righteousness of Jesus, and a new obedience brought about by the Holy Spirit. We talked of his sin and of Jesus's death to forgive that sin. We talked of Jesus's unmerited promise of saving grace, and this young boy called on the name of the Lord for salvation.

Ultimately, this young boy was not saved because his mother was a Christian and took him to church a time or two. He was not saved because of the eloquence of my words. This boy was saved because, in the fullness of time, the Spirit of God moved in his heart to bring conviction of sin and to draw him to Jesus. Yes, our God works through families, but families do not constrain Him. Children (and grown-ups) from non-Christian families are saved every day. The grace of God saves them through the working of the Spirit in their lives. This is beautifully true and is evident in the lives of many who are reading this book. But it is also true that God has sovereignly chosen to work through the covenant family.

Our hope is in the covenant-making God who has kept His covenant promise in and through the person and work of Jesus Christ. Our call as parents is to set an environment within the family where our children know from the earliest ages what is most important to us. We teach our children the Word. We pray for them and with them. We set an example for them of godliness and humble gospel dependence. And we do this because our highest calling as parents is to point our children to a personal relationship with Jesus.

What Does It Matter?

We spend time on God's covenant of grace because none of us qualify as jam-up parents when it comes to our children's salvation. If we solely focus on parenting techniques, we are likely to give rise to children who are either blindly robotic or hopelessly rebellious. As parents, we will become neurotic in our actions or locked up in fear.

When we trust that the Word of God is true, we find hope. Our hope is not in our techniques. Our hope is not in the responsiveness or politeness of our children. Our hope is in the God who has graciously promised the Redeemer and who has declared that through the Redeemer, we would be His people. Praise the Lord!

We cling to hope by trusting in God's covenant promise, and then we raise our children considering that promise. It impacts how we talk to and teach our children, understanding they are not strangers to God. They are His people. It impacts the way we include them in worship and, ultimately, the value we see in our children, understanding they, too, are recipients of the promise. We presume upon the promise, and we pray in accord with the promise that God will sovereignly, graciously, mercifully move in their hearts.

God's covenant promise is a tangible reminder that He is at work in the world and in our families. With this truth rooted in our hearts, we can rest in worship. In Romans, this is where Paul ultimately goes. After wrestling with the identity of God's covenant people, in Romans 11:33–36, he finally breaks out in song. Even amid all its challenges, parenting considering God's covenant promise gives us the ability to sing along.

> Oh, the depth of the riches and wisdom and knowledge of God! How unsearchable are his judgments and how inscrutable his ways!

"For who has known the mind of the Lord,
or who has been his counselor?"
"Or who has given a gift to him
that he might be repaid?"

For from him and through him and to him are all
things. To him be glory forever. Amen.

CHAPTER 6

Parenting as Stewardship

Pointing to the Rightful Owner

The earth is the LORD's and the fullness thereof,
the world and those who dwell therein.

—Psalm 24:1

My oldest son and my daughter have my brown eyes and
their mother's red hair. Friends will tell us my son looks like
me and my daughter looks like my wife. They are a perfect
combination of the two of us in appearance and temperament.
My youngest son is different. He has blonde hair and blue
eyes. But I located one of my baby pictures which bears *some*
resemblance to him.

All families share these resemblances of features and
temperament. Ours is no different. These similarities give
me much enjoyment, though my boys are beginning to look
at my receding hairline with a sense of impending doom. I
remind them I had plenty of hair before they were born, but
that's beside the point.

While these similarities are a gift from the Lord displaying our connectedness within the family, they can have the negative effect of furthering an unhelpful story line: that our children belong to *us*. Yet, God's Word points to a very different story line based on a different ownership structure. A deeper, truer similarity points to our ultimate source of belonging. In Genesis 1:27, God's Word points us to our primary likeness.

> So God created man in his own image,
> in the image of God he created him;
> male and female He created them.

My children may look like me, but they were made in God's image.

Parenting as Stewards

At its most basic level, stewardship is a matter of ownership, defining who is the owner and who is the steward. By definition, a steward manages the property of another. In this case, the *another* is God, and the *property* is our children.

Maybe it sounds a little crass to think of our precious children as property. That would certainly be true if we were talking about the owner as a slave trader. But here that is certainly not the case. We are talking about the Lord God Almighty, maker of heaven and earth, the God who has chosen to define His relationship with His redeemed people using the word *Father*.

In addition to Father, our God is the King of Glory. In Psalm 24:1, a psalm which in my Bible carries the title "The King of Glory," we are reminded of this truth: "The earth is the LORD's and the fullness thereof, the world and those who dwell therein." All belong to the Lord. He owns parent and child. That's right, the Lord also owns us as parents. We belong, body and soul, to the Lord and are called to steward our very lives for the glory of God.

Therefore, when we speak of parenting as stewards, we are reminded that God Himself is our children's rightful owner and that, for a time, He has chosen to entrust them to our care. Stewardship, by definition, is a matter of ownership, and ownership, by definition, establishes authority.

Ownership Establishes Authority

I usually think of my children's strong wills as a good thing. On my not-so-good days, I tend to use different adjectives. I know and trust their wills will serve them well, but currently they can be a challenge!

To shape their wills from a young age, my call as a steward *over* them is to establish an authority structure *for* them. The biblical call, I believe, is to establish firm authority structures while not acting in an authoritarian way (see Ephesians 6:1–4). As parents, we must be reminded that we are under authority. Those lines of authority begin to take shape when we understand not only that our children are not our own but also that *we are not our own.*

Our authority over our children as their parents (which scripture clearly speaks to in the fifth commandment) falls under the Lord's authority over us. Again, we are acting as His stewards in our role as parents. When I shape my children's beautifully strong wills, I am establishing my authority, ultimately by pointing them to the source of *all* authority. As the owner of all, our God has authority over all, including authority over our parenting.

Ownership Establishes Goals

In addition to establishing authority, ownership also establishes our goals, which is fundamental to our understanding of parenting. If I am a steward, my goal in parenting can't merely be to raise my children so that they don't embarrass me in public. Many of us struggle with the widespread fear that our children will act out in public, either with or without us.

Without consciously thinking about it, those fears come from an ownership mindset. If my children belong to me, their obedience (or lack thereof) reflects on me and far too often drives my search for self-worth. If our goal is to raise our children so they don't embarrass us, these failures can seem horrifying. We should shape for obedience, but ultimately that is a matter of pursuing their hearts more than maintaining our reputations.

Instead, I believe God's Word tells us our fundamental goal in parenting is to point our children to their rightful owner. In parenting as a steward, our primary goal is to present our children to the Lord. This truth gives context to the calling of parenthood: discipleship. In discipleship, we are called to point our children to the beauty of Jesus.

Parenting as a steward is not detached parenting! It is not heartless or loveless. I adore my children. As I write, all three are teenagers. And we have a blast together. I enjoy being with them, and they (most of the time) enjoy being with my wife and me.

The point is I adore them and enjoy being with them so much that I intend to be with them for all of eternity! My goal in pointing them to the grace of the Lord Jesus Christ is meant to glorify God as I speak of my love for Him. But it is also meant to point them to a relationship with Jesus that we can share for all eternity. My love for them, my *delight* in them, is at the very core of my discipleship of them.

Freedom in Stewardship

In addition to understanding the goal of parenting, I am also beginning to see beautiful, gospel freedom resulting from my understanding of my children's rightful owner. This truth gives me freedom from trying to use them to establish my identity.

In my town, youth sports are our favorite pastime. I've described my town as a college town without a college. Life revolves around high school sports, but those high school sports have a way of trickling down to the youngest children. As you drive the streets of our town, you pass countless homes where parents are out in their yards coaching their children.

There is beauty in this parental involvement, but it can also have a dark underbelly. At the baseball park, for example, I am amazed at the decibel level surrounding the five- and six-year-old fields. Most of the noise is cheering. But some of the noise comes from a different form of yelling.

What drives this passion and anger toward six-year-old baseball players? Some of it is that we just love to cheer for our kids. Some of it is that we are looking for our kids to form our identity. If they excel in anything, then we are affirmed. We have a sense of self-worth.

That is the story line we often create for ourselves, but the story line of Scripture tells us something different. Our kids belong to the Lord. Their identity is *Him*. They may look like us, but they are created in His image, and though we have marred it by our sin, Jesus is redeeming His image. That same truth of identity in Christ holds for us as parents. When we understand this, we can be free from looking to our children for things they were never meant to provide, namely our sense of self-worth.

I see this clearly in others at the ballpark. But the truth is I struggle in the same ways in other places, and I can confidently assume that you do too. Wherever and whenever we feel this temptation to place our worth in our children, we should constantly go back to the gospel. We should continually remind ourselves that we are not our own and that Christ has bought us. He is our hope. And He is our children's hope.

Freedom to Nurture Their Gifting

Another freedom comes when we understand that we are parenting as stewards. When we grasp that our children have been created by God and have been uniquely gifted by God, we find the freedom to nurture their gifting rather than trying to define that gifting for them.

One of the things we like to do in our family is to take trips with our kids. Trips together build a sense of adventure, allow us to enjoy one another, and serve as a great foundation for future meaningful conversations. Early on, I began to envision trips I would take with my boys. I love to be outside and have always enjoyed the rare hunting and fishing trips I've been able to take. In my mind those hunting and fishing trips would be fantastic with the boys. But they like to visit cities.

Their idea of a perfect getaway involves a city and some form of professional sports. Their interests differ from mine, but the Lord has given me the grace to embrace this. Rather than force the issue and re-create them in my image, the Lord has given me the freedom to nurture their preferences. And on those trips, we've had a great time together.

These varying interests point to a deeper spiritual truth. For His glory and the blessing of His church, God gifts His children uniquely with differing spiritual gifts. Those gifts come from the Lord, and He means for us as parents to nurture those unique gifts in our children. When we parent as stewards, we need to know what our gifting is and what it is not. It is just as important to know the same about our children.

This may sound odd, but it means we parent like a pastor. In Ephesians 4:11–12, we are told that God gave us pastors to equip the saints for the work of ministry. When you parent like a pastor, you help your children identify and nurture their gifts for service in the kingdom of God. That doesn't mean you are preparing them for vocational ministry. It doesn't mean you are trying to raise little missionaries. It means you are training them up to live into their unique God-given gifting.

Personally, this truth challenges me to give my children to the Lord. I have hopes and dreams for my children, but I don't own them or control them. God does, and in His wisdom, He has given them to me for a season to nurture and enjoy. Ultimately, my role as a parent is to give them to the Lord.

Abraham and Isaac

Genesis 22 offers a graphic illustration of this truth. The story of Abraham and Isaac contains one that challenges my micromanagement and ownership approach to my children. It is a story that terrifies me until I get to a conclusion.

I've read Genesis 22 countless times, but a play in my former town brought it all to life for me. An intimate little downtown theater in Greensboro, North Carolina, called Triad Stage has produced a play titled *Beautiful Star: An Appalachian Nativity*. One of the play's scenes recounted God's instructions to Abraham to sacrifice his only son, Isaac.

I've seen the play several times, but this one scene always grips me. The actor who played the part of Abraham captured the fullness of his emotion beautifully. Abraham didn't understand this instruction from his Lord, but he was obedient. He loved his son dearly but understood that the boy belonged to the Lord. In anguish, he gave his son over to the Lord, not understanding but trusting the perfect word of the Lord.

In this intimate playhouse, the audience sitting on top of the stage could sense every bit of the drama. Isaac, bound by his daddy, didn't understand but trusted. Then just as Abraham was about to plunge the knife, the Lord stopped him. I know the end of the story, but I am still undone.

The tension of this drama can leave us questioning God, that is, if we don't know the end of the story. How could *this* God be trustworthy? How could I be expected to point my child to *this* God if He would seem to be this cavalier with His requests of me and my parenting? Is *this* the kind of God who is worthy of owning *my* child?

If we simply stop at Genesis 22:12, it might seem appropriate to ask these questions about the goodness and trustworthiness of God. But we don't stop there. The Lord provided a ram for Abraham to sacrifice that day because on another day His son would serve as the sacrifice.

Isaac was, in a real sense, brought back from the dead (Hebrews 11:19) because Jesus would go to His death and be raised for us. The Father sent Him there because He was the only hope to redeem sinful man. And the Father raised Him in glory, where He now sits, praying for us. This is the kind of Father we have! This kind of Father owns our children and has given us the privilege of caring for them.

God's ownership of all things and all people is a foundational truth of Scripture. It is also a foundational truth of our parenting. Yes, our children may look like us. Yes, for better or worse, sometimes they even act like us. But they were created in the image of God. Our highest calling as parents is to prepare them for their rightful owner.

CHAPTER 7

It Takes the Church

God's Perfect Wisdom for Redemptive Community

So then you are no longer strangers and aliens, but you are fellow citizens with the saints and members of the household of God, built on the foundation of the apostles and prophets, Christ Jesus himself being the cornerstone, in whom the whole structure, being joined together, grows into a holy temple in the Lord. In him you also are being built together into a dwelling place for God by the Spirit.

—Ephesians 2:19–22

Submitting to one another out of reverence for Christ.

—Ephesians 5:21

65

I've recently been teaching our youngest son how to drive a car. At this point, we have somewhat of a routine for these driving instructions. One of my standard lessons for the kids is to teach them about blind spots. It is an important lesson to pass on because, unlike other skills required in driving that they know they need to master, they are completely oblivious to blind spots.

Usually as we drive down the road, I'll make a quick check to ensure the coast is clear, and then I'll instruct them to change lanes. You know what happens next. They may take a quick look in the mirror. They may even use their blinker. But they never turn back to check the blind spot.

We then pull into the next available parking lot. I get out of the car, walk over to the blind spot, and tell them to look in the mirror to see if they see me. Bam! I've got them. They had no idea a car could be beside them, hidden from the side-view mirror. Oh, they'll need more reminding, but from that point on, they know they need to turn and look before changing lanes.

Did you know we have blind spots in life as well? Life's blind spots are more difficult to overcome than the ones in our driving because when driving you know exactly where the blind spot is located. The problem with blind spots in life is that you don't even know you have them! Hence the name. We all have places in our lives, beliefs, or actions where we are oblivious to our faults and false convictions. Not knowing where they are, we can't simply turn back to look for dangerous objects. We need others in our lives who will do the looking for us.

For these others to be effective blind-spot catchers, we must give them enough access to know us. They need to be mature friends who not only know us but also know and love Jesus. Finally, we must experience a relationship where they have the freedom and responsibility to lovingly speak truth into the deeper recesses of our hearts. We need these types of friends, but we also need to extend this type of friendship to others. Where can we find these others? The church is the most appropriate place for us to find these special friends and to be that kind of friend for them.

The Wisdom of God

Maybe you're asking yourself why we're including the church in a portion of this book focused on foundations of belief. Maybe you're thinking you take your kids to church, but beyond that, what does the church have to do with our parenting? To answer that question, we need to answer a fundamental question about the church. Is the church an invention of man, added on to biblical Christianity? Or is the church central to God's design for the life, growth, and blessing of the Christian? Is the church meant to give the Christian a context to more fully enjoy a relationship with God *now* and to more comprehensively prepare the Christian for an eternally glorious relationship with God *later*?

I'm trying to draw a stark contrast to expose the implications. Scripture clearly points to the church as God's eternal design for the Christian life. The church is the bride of Christ. The church is the dwelling place for God by the Spirit. The church is the wisdom of God. With these truths in mind, can we be honest with ourselves for a few moments about how we have practically approached the church?

Going to Church vs. Being the Church

How many of us think in terms of *going to church*? Many of us describe the church as a place we go for a weekly service. While there, we might hear something helpful. We might be encouraged. And then we go back and live our lives.

That approach to church sounds like going to a movie. What happens when you go to a movie? You drive to the theater and buy a ticket. You go in and sit down in a room full of strangers. There you receive a service (entertainment), and then you leave. And with technology, you can *do the movies* at home.

When we speak of going to church, is it really all that different from going to the movies? Many churches facilitate this through a customer service orientation, catering to our desires, but this isn't the biblical definition of the church. When we buy into this model, we miss out on the blessing Jesus has planned for us. If going to church isn't the biblical model for the church, how about another? Being the church.

Biblically, the church is not a compartmentalized destination. It is a description of our being. We are the church. We are the bride of Christ. Rather than the *go to the movies* model, maybe a more helpful picture is the family meal. What happens when the extended family gathers for a meal? Sometimes it's loud and messy. But there is also laughter. There is mutual serving as we pass the dishes down the table. We care for the kids at the children's table. We listen to our uncles' stories. There is love.

I know we have baggage when we consider the church. We also have baggage when we consider the extended family. But even when we have not experienced joy on these occasions, we instinctively know that family is meant to be joyous. And that reminds us that this gathering for the family meal is a gathering of the new family. In the new family of the redeemed, all are included: singles, marrieds, widows, and orphans. And in this family, there is commitment, care, love, and submission.

The church of Jesus Christ is not a collection of individuals who gather to receive a service. Instead, it is a Spirit-filled, Spirit-fueled new family gathered as the church in a series of mutually dependent relationships where we experience the blessing of intimacy with God and one another. Instead of going to church, we need to be the church.

But some may still be asking what this has to do with our parenting. Well, we need this mutual commitment in our lives to shape and point us to Jesus. The church is the relational context for a Christ-centered life of mutual submission and love. It is God's wisdom for the Christian life, and through it, the Holy Spirit will grow us and our parenting.

Our children are also blessed and shaped by the beauty of the church. In this loving and committed context, they learn that submission is good. They learn to love and be loved by other flawed human beings. In short, through the church they grow in Christlikeness.

What Holds Us Back?

For some, we've never heard of this model of the church. We've grown up with a cultural expectation that we are to go to church on Sunday morning, but we left it there. But the Word of God opens us up to a bigger, more beautiful design for the blessing of mutual commitment and submission in the context of God's design and wisdom for the church.

Others of us may hear and even be interested in going deeper with the family of Christ, but we're busy. We've got vacation homes and ball games. Some of us are struggling with the competing desires that keep us from committing and submitting to the family of Christ. What might it look like to reconsider where the family of Christ fits into our priorities?

There are others of us whom the church has burned. Some hear about this picture of the church and think that sounds good, but we've been hurt before. We'll come, but we've got to protect ourselves and hold the church at a safe distance. We can't mutually submit because that didn't work last time.

Sadly, the hurt can happen again. But we can take comfort in knowing that many of the New Testament letters were written to messed-up churches, pointing them back to the gospel. We can take comfort in knowing that God's design is for our good and that He works through the hurt, desiring our whole hearts.

The Check Engine Light

This biblical picture of the church is a beautiful call to a life of submission within the body of Christ. The Word of God commands us to mutually submit to one another in the context of the church (Ephesians 5:21), but this submission, like most other commands in scripture, can serve as a check engine light for our relationship with Jesus. When the check engine light comes on, it's indicative of the car needing an oil change. Other times we need routine maintenance, or we have serious, engine-threatening problems. To find the underlying cause of the light and determine what is going on, we need to look under the hood.

If we consider ourselves to be Christians but are not living lives of mutual commitment and submission within the family of Christ (not being the church), we likely need to "check under the hood." Our lack of commitment and submission serves as a check engine light shining on the dashboard of our hearts. When we see that light, we need to look under the hood to consider where we might be missing out on biblical discipleship and the beauty of the gospel.

The biblical call to be the church exposes much within us. It also invites us to look under the hood that we might find a life of meaning, purpose, and blessing.

It Takes a Village

Please don't think to yourself for one moment that this is easier for a pastor's family. On top of all the other cultural struggles we encounter, add the issue of expectation. Our kids didn't wake up early on Sunday mornings pleasantly whistling with anticipation at the thought of gathering with the church family to worship. There were times when they simply wanted to sleep. There are still times when we have competing desires. But in our better moments, we lean into the struggle and discuss it openly with our kids.

This is what parenting is all about. Rather than following our children's desires, we lead. But before we can lead, we must be confident in the foundational truth behind our parenting/leadership. The church is God's design for our blessing, for our growth in Christlikeness, and for His glory. In the church, we live in the blessing of mutually dependent relationships across the generational spectrum where together we are looking to Christ.

The church is a family (thus the foundational precept of this book), and we get the blessing of mutual love and care in this family. Those of us who are already parents know by now that we need help. Those who are not yet parents will come to learn that lesson soon.

A large part of that help is the blessing of other voices speaking into our children's lives with the same gospel message. We need young adults in their twenties and thirties who lovingly care for our teenagers and model healthy, Christ-dependent relationships for them. We will want teenagers, as messy as they can be, to come alongside our younger children. We will want the wisdom of older adults for our sanity and for our children's sake. We want other voices speaking into our children's lives, as this multiplies the moments of gospel application they experience. We find this through our committed membership in the local church. It is one of the highest priorities for our family life. This blessing was revealed as our oldest son graduated from high school. He had many close friendships among his high school classmates, but when it came time for us to throw a graduation party, he wanted his church family there with him. When we asked him about it, he told us that those people, across the age spectrum, had loved him and spoken into his life.

My wife and I reflected on those relationships and realized that through many of the difficult teenage experiences, this church family had come alongside our son and cared for him, incarnating the gospel of Jesus Christ. Though we didn't realize how important the local church was to the spiritual growth of our family, the Spirit of God was working through the church to bless our children.

The local church is the priority that will bear lasting fruit in the lives of our children. God's design is for real-life, messy, intergenerational churches where believers "do life together" and grow together in Christ. The church is a foundational tenet of God's design for the Christian life and must be a foundational belief of our parenting.

Section 2

The Construction

Principles of Practice

> *I am the good shepherd. I know my own and my own know me.*
>
> —John 10:14

Christmas cards, the kind you receive in the mail, seem to be a quickly fading annual treat. Though the social media posts replacing them can be a lot of fun, I miss the excitement of my December mailbox run. Yet a few holdouts remain.

One Christmas card sticks out from our past as I try to conjure up an image of the model family. This family is a take-your-breath-away-beautiful kind of family, all of them. They don't even look real. It's as if they are the product of a modeling agency talent search.

Their picture is usually taken in some exotic place. The grandchildren are all smiling and well dressed. But it's not merely the picture. When you look, you are reminded that these are extraordinary people. The adults are all accomplished professionals, and the grandchildren do well in school and appear well-mannered. It's quite something. We would always flip through the stack of Christmas cards, looking for that one.

These friends are all fantastic people and have a great family. But should they be the model as we consider how to parent our children? No! It's not that there is anything wrong with our Christmas card family. It's just that you and I may not be able to produce that picture-perfect image or that family.

OK, so where do we look for a model family? Television has tried to offer some thoughts. In the 1950s and early 1960s, Hollywood gave us *Leave It to Beaver* and *Father Knows Best*. Those shows have given way over the years to *The Waltons*, *The Cosby Show*, and now, *Modern Family*. The message now seems to be the normality of divorce, cross-generational remarriage, gay marriage, and children who often possess more wisdom than their parents.

A Scriptural Model for the Family

My point is not necessarily to bash culture but to ask where we are to find a model for the family and our parenting. If it's not found in our Christmas cards or television programming, the best place for us to look is in the Scriptures. Yet at first glance, that also appears problematic. Where in Scripture do we see the prototype?

Adam and Eve? Well, no. There was the whole Cain and Abel matter. Abraham, Isaac, and Jacob? I don't think so. Their family stories are one mess after another. How about David? He was a man used mightily by God, but I don't think we want to model our family life and parenting after him. Do you remember the saga of adultery, murder, and deceit blowing up into a family feud that led to a civil war?

As we go down the list of Bible families, I haven't found a shining example of the model Christian family. And that makes me think we are looking for the wrong thing. Should we even be looking for a model? Or at least a picture of a family we are called to emulate? We may be asking the wrong question. Instead of a picture-perfect, Christmas card family, perhaps we should simply be looking for principles to guide our parenting. If that's the case, maybe the model family isn't a family at all, or at least not as we usually think of one. Maybe the model family is the church.

What is the church? It is the bride of Christ. It is the covenant community. It is the family of God. Is it perfect? No way! Is it redeemed? Yes! Is it being transformed? Yes! The church is a beautiful mess, much like your two-year-old. And the church is probably the best model in Scripture for the Christian family. At least, it is the best that I can think of.

I'm not talking about the specific local church to which you may be united, though I pray it shares these marks. I'm talking about the church as designed and presented in Scripture. The church in Acts was a place of grace where people were committed to one another and were led by God-appointed leaders who cared for their people. It was a place of mutual love, submission, and care. It was a place centered on a joint mission. It was a place—or rather a community of people (family)—wholly given over to the worship of their Lord and Savior. And I would submit that this picture of the early church in Acts was not some Norman Rockwell picture meant to make us feel nostalgic. Instead, I believe it is intended to show us the faithful, timeless church.

Jesus connected the church with the family by speaking of her as His bride. Paul then used the family as an illustration of the church in Ephesians. In Ephesians chapter 5, after speaking of the love, submission, and selfless sacrifice that exists in a marriage, he went on in verse 32 to say, "This mystery is profound, and I am saying that it refers to Christ and the church." Paul's very next topic then dealt with parenting.

The church isn't perfect. The accounts of the church in the New Testament paint a messy picture. While the local church may be a place of great blessing, it can also be a place of pain. This is to be expected as we are not yet perfected in glory. I'm not pointing to the church as many of us may have experienced it as a model for the family but rather to the church as it was designed.

If we can go with this point, let's move on to the application in terms of our parenting. My assertion is this: if the church is the model family, the elder should be an appropriate model for our parenting.

Learning to Shepherd from the Good Shepherd

I grew up on a farm, at least in my early years, and I still love to go back. My earliest and best memories were often from my time with my father, grandfather, and uncles, working with the cows. Most Saturdays were spent doing some form of work on the farm. After all, the cows needed to be cared for.

Our farm work included feeding the cows, cutting and bringing in the hay, repairing fences, moving cows from one field to another, and tending to their various medical needs. All those tasks could be summed up into two major categories: (1) nurturing their healthy growth by providing for their needs (that is, feeding them) and (2) keeping them from whatever harm they might do to themselves or that might come their way (that is, protecting them).

Though I always thought of the shepherds as the kids with sticks in the Christmas play, our farm work was a modern-day form of shepherding. We cared for cows instead of sheep, but the basic premise was the same. It is a premise of care, woven into the fabric of Scripture and displaying God's design for the church elder.

In Genesis 2:15, God gave Adam an elementary job description. He placed Adam in the garden of Eden to work it and to keep it. In short, God commanded Adam to nurture and cultivate the garden and to protect it from harm. These are the primary tasks of a shepherd. In the 23rd Psalm, we are told through poetry that this is how our Lord shepherds us.

The Lord, our shepherd, nurtures His children through His gracious provision, as seen in verses 1–3:

> The Lord is my shepherd; I shall not want.
> He makes me lie down in green pastures.
> He leads me beside still waters.
> He restores my soul.
> He leads me in paths of righteousness
> for his name's sake.

Then, we see our Shepherd protecting His sheep from harm in verse 4:

> Even though I walk through the valley of the
> shadow of death,
> I will fear no evil,
> for you are with me;
> your rod and your staff,
> they comfort me.

Finally, in verses 5 and 6, we see the Lord's gracious blessing through a combination of His feeding and protecting:

> You prepare a table before me
> in the presence of my enemies;

you anoint my head with oil;
my cup overflows.
Surely goodness and mercy shall follow me
all the days of my life,
and I shall dwell in the house of the LORD
forever.

It is a beautiful picture of the Lord's loving care for His children. It helps us see the gift of provision He has given regarding the church's leadership. This is the role of the elder in the church of Jesus Christ: to feed the people of God and to protect them from wolves. We can begin to see more clearly what is meant by the elder as an appropriate model for our parenting.

Given this picture of parenting, we should have a relatively easy job. It boils down to two tasks. Nurture them and protect them, though these two tasks are not simple. They imply much. We are not simply nurturing and protecting them so they will grow physically. We are nurturing and protecting their hearts. At the same time, we need our hearts to be nurtured and protected!

Where do we turn for help? We turn to the Good Shepherd. Jesus is not primarily our role model. Jesus is primarily our Savior, which was made clear in our gospel primer in chapter 3. However, there is much we can learn from Jesus in the way He shepherds us.

Beyond what we read in the 23rd Psalm, we get a glimpse into Jesus's shepherding as we look at how He cared for the disciples. He shepherded these men whom He would later commission to go and build the church. Yes, He was their Savior, but He was also their discipling mentor.

While we aren't Jesus, I believe there are some important principles we can glean from His shepherding which should inform our parenting. This is where we go now. Think of them as principles of practice. If the basics of belief formed the doctrinal foundation of our parenting, the principles of practice are more of the philosophy of construction we employ as we build on the foundation.

As we look to Jesus's shepherding, there are four of these principles which serve as a helpful framework for our parenting: engage, delight, shape, and pray.

In the coming chapters, we will expand on this assertion that the church is the appropriate model for the family, leading us to see the elder as the appropriate model for our parenting. In doing so, we will see how these four principles, taken from Jesus's shepherding, can bless our parenting.

CHAPTER 8

Engage

The Principle of "Being With"

And he appointed twelve (whom he also named apostles) so that they might be with him and he might send them out to preach and have authority to cast out demons.

—Mark 3:14–15

My earliest and best memories took place on Saturday mornings. Growing up on the farm, there was always work to do, yet it hardly ever felt like work. Maybe that is because my brother and I got to be with the most influential men in our lives: my father, grandfather, and uncles.

No Saturday was the same, but given the distance of memory, a general pattern prevailed. We gathered at the barn. There was some small talk, sketching a general plan for the day, and then we loaded up in the truck. But we weren't headed out to work yet. We went to the gas station in search of fuel for our bellies.

Though I don't recommend the diet (and haven't carried this on with my children), my Saturday morning fuel consisted of a Coca-Cola and a pack of white confectionary sugar doughnuts. I can still taste them! Armed for the day, we then returned to the barn, got our gear together, and rode out for the day's chores.

Some days we were mending fences. Some days we were moving cows from one field to the next. Some days we were cutting hay, and on others we cut wood. The form of work didn't matter to me. What mattered most was that I had been invited into the fellowship of the menfolk.

As a young boy, I didn't know how to capture that feeling with words. I didn't have to. I just knew their strength, and I knew it felt right. I was being taught, sometimes with words, sometimes with actions, and always within the bond of men who cared for one another and me.

There is something else I didn't know how to communicate back then, and I'm not sure if my father did either. It just seemed to come naturally on the farm, as I've seen from other farm families as well. The men were training me. Or as we call it in Christian circles, they were discipling me. Yet, their training/discipleship began with a relationship.

I wasn't productive on those Saturday mornings, but I was *with*. I can remember sitting on my father's lap, steering the tractor. He didn't need me to drive. Quite frankly, I added no productive value to this crew. But he had me *with* him. They had me *with* them. And in *being with*, I was growing into something more.

Be With

Those Saturday mornings were foundational for me. They were good. They were true. They were beautiful. And like all things which are good, true, and beautiful, those Saturday mornings were in some way a reflection of the God who is good, true, and beautiful. I doubt that the men in my family searched the Scriptures for a model of how to raise me, but those Saturday mornings were biblical, nonetheless.

In Mark 3, Jesus appointed the twelve apostles. He had been ministering with these men already, but Mark 3 is the point at which things were made official. It was as if Jesus was having the DTR (define the relationship) conversation with them. And in recording the event, I believe Mark is explicitly pulling out an element of Jesus's discipleship which is only noted more implicitly in the other gospel accounts. Remember, we're building principles of practice for our parenting based on how Jesus shepherded and discipled the disciples and, by extension, the church. The principle Mark made clear in Mark 3:14–15 is that discipleship is a relationship before it is an activity.

In these two verses, Jesus made it clear what He would do with the disciples as He trained them to go and build the church. With that in mind, it is astonishingly beautiful that the first order of business for Jesus was that the disciples would be with Him. This is the first reason for Jesus's appointment: "so that they might be with him" (Mark 3:14). This took priority. Then secondly, He appointed them so that He might send them out to preach and have the authority to cast out demons.

One of the primary methods of Jesus's shepherding care was to be with these men. Don't you see? That is precisely what was happening on those Saturday mornings long ago. My father, grandfather, and uncles would one day send me off to do chores on my own. I would grow in responsibility, knowledge, and stature. But it started with and would remain dependent upon a relationship that in its simplest form could be described as "being with."

As I have looked at Jesus's shepherding model and considered its implications for my parenting, I've tried to capture all of this with one word: *engage*. To *engage* certainly means to be with, but I believe it means more. Jesus wasn't just hanging out with the disciples, though I am sure His being with them certainly included moments of sitting around the campfire. It was that, but it was also intentional.

To *engage* means to be with and, in the context of being with, it means to talk about things that matter and to share experiences that matter. This talking with and sharing with are ways we model for our children how we are to remain with Jesus as He is engaging us.

Talk About Things That Matter

What should we talk to our children about? It depends on their ages. Whatever their age, we need to talk about the things that interest them. Those things may be baby dolls or puppy dogs. They may be bicycles or swimming lessons. It may be tee ball. It may be their friends or their boyfriends and girlfriends. It may be college football.

Wherever they are, know them there. Know the influences in their lives. Know about their friends. Know about their activities. But most importantly, learn about their hearts.

As I grow older, I notice that I have some relationships where I just can't seem to go beneath the surface. Our conversations generally revolve around ball games, and we seem resort to small talk, which I despise. But sometimes, I don't know how to get beyond it. Perhaps it's because I've got some relationships where I've been trained to stay in those safe areas. I pray that'll never be true with my kids.

But how do we go deeper with our kids? I think it starts by developing a sense of curiosity about them. The more curious we are about their hearts, the more penetrating we will be with our questions. Recently I heard this put another way: "Never stop being a student of your child's heart."

Again, we learn from Jesus. Later in Mark 8:27, Jesus was walking down the road with His disciples. As they walked, He asked them a question. "Who do people say that I am?" It was a straightforward question, but it only required them to relay facts they had heard from other people. Those facts were interesting, but Jesus wanted something more. He wanted to know them. Therefore, He asked a more personal question: "Who do you say that I am?" (Mark 8:29).

Jesus engaged with the disciples by talking with them. As He spoke with them, He continued to lean in, making the conversation more and more personal. We do the same when we do more than engage our kids about their stats in the basketball game. We also ask how it felt when the coach yanked them out of the game after one small mistake. We talk to them about their fear of dogs or their fear of failure. We speak to them about their joy over making the grade.

A big part of talking about things that matter is peeling back the layers of facts and figures so that we can pursue our children's hearts. As parents, we should be doing this regardless of the subject matter. But another part of talking about what matters is intentionally going to the hard subjects.

Ball games are all well and good. Some of my best memories with my children have been the exciting moments we have enjoyed together over sports. But those games cannot be the extent of our subject matter. We must talk to our children about things of lasting consequence. We must speak to them about the hard things they are experiencing or that their friends are experiencing. We must speak with them about their hopes and dreams. We must speak to them about sex and marriage. We must speak to them about pornography. We must speak with them about the gospel.

These topics are weighty. They may even be scary, but as parents who are called to engage with our children, we enter in. And we don't wait until our children become older teenagers before we address these challenging topics. My wife and I got this wake-up call when our oldest son was in the fourth grade. While on a school field trip, he was exposed to pornography.

Thankfully, he told us about it. We were shocked and realized it was time to have "the talk." I was clumsy and awkward. It was painfully obvious that neither he nor I wanted to be around for this discussion. And that realization taught me something. First, my wife and I realized that this was not a one-time discussion. Second, we learned that the more we engage with our children by talking about things that matter, the more we will continue engaging them with things that matter.

I may be writing now, but I'm still figuring these things out. I'm still learning to see the wisdom of Jesus and to trust that He loves my children even more than I do. I am learning to pray over my past mistakes and to continue praying for future wisdom. Through those prayers, He is showing me much. In this call to talk about things that matter, I am seeing two important points, which I am trying to include more and more.

First, as we learn from Jesus about engaging with our children, we must learn how to make the Word of God a natural part of the discussion. We'll talk about some specific application points later, but for now, it is essential to see that we need to include Scripture in our conversations with our children. Our kids need to know that we don't only bring the Bible out when we are doing a formal lesson. They need to see that it speaks into their everyday lives. Honestly, most of us need the reminder to make the Word a natural part of our lives together.

To do so, the Word of God must be a part of our everyday life. My pastoral ministry is informed more by my personal devotional life than by specific teaching points I received in seminary. We need an overall framework to understand Scripture. It's also helpful to be prepared in advance for specific situations that might arise. But daily, the Lord will provide what we need for our parenting as we feed on the Word of God.

Secondly, make honesty and vulnerability a natural part of the discussion. There is undoubtedly an age appropriateness to this, but our children need to know that we need Jesus. We model much for our children when we acknowledge our needs before them. This may mean we need to ask for their forgiveness. Other times, this means we are trying to teach them to learn from our mistakes. Both have an excellent way of drawing our children and us closer together and pointing our children to Jesus. Often, I've had to tell my children, "Dad needs Jesus too." Statements like this have a way of positioning us side by side, together looking to the cross.

Share Experiences That Matter

It's vital we talk about things that matter, but it is equally important that we share experiences that matter. Shared experiences make memories, and memories shape future values. Sharing experiences requires an element of selflessness. It requires sharing, so you must want to share in your children's experiences and have them share in yours.

Again, we are looking to Jesus for our model. In Luke chapter 22, we have one of the accounts of the Lord's Supper. Similar accounts are found in Matthew 26, Mark 14, and 1 Corinthians 11, but Luke pulls out a beautiful nuance. In Luke 22:15, he captures Jesus's words, "I have earnestly desired to eat this Passover with you before I suffer."

Isn't that beautiful? Jesus is about to go to the cross, but first, He earnestly desires to share a meal with His disciples. He is sharing an experience that matters. He desires to celebrate the Passover meal. Passover was a meal celebrating God's faithfulness in redeeming His people, and Jesus wanted to share it with His friends, all before He became the Passover Lamb. He was remembering, and He was giving meaning. It would be one of those times they would look back on that would shape their future values, and ours.

Jesus's life together with the disciples was all about shared experiences that mattered. They lived together. They were on a mission together. They taught together. They fed thousands together. He brought the closest of His friends along to see His glory in the transfiguration and to pray with Him.

With this lead-in, our shared experiences all seem lesser. Maybe, but there is a principle that is no less important in the lives of our family. Some of those shared experiences were significant events. Others were daily life. All mattered.

When we think about engaging with our children over shared experiences, we need to know that some will be scripted, but most will not. We won't always know when a memory is being made, but if we are intentional about "being with," our lives together will be rich with memories.

Shared experiences that matter come in all shapes and sizes. Some are big, and others are small. Friday nights in our home fall into the little category. It doesn't happen all the time, but occasionally we will have pizza night, only our pizza nights have evolved. As the kids got older, it became more expensive to order out, so we had to come up with another option.

While my wife, Anna, carries more than her share of the load in the kitchen throughout the week, I generally try to give her some help on the weekends. One Father's Day, I received a pizza stone and dough-making lessons. At that point, our Friday pizza nights took on a whole new flavor.

We have a deal. When I cook, I want the kids around. Usually, my daughter is the DJ, playing her latest favorite songs. The boys float in and out, but they don't stray too far because they want a say in what goes on the pizza. There is nothing magical about the pizza. There is usually nothing magical about the conversation. But we are together, and they love pizza nights. It has become our family's identifying mark, drawing us together. And that ultimately is the goal. Our relationship will lead to greater opportunities for meaning and depth, but it begins with "being with."

While some experiences that matter consist of eating a meal together, others flow out of opportunities to serve our neighbors. For us, this shows up in the church. While my wife and kids are not church employees, church planting is a family affair. It has been an adventure, far bigger (and more difficult) than anything we could have imagined. There have been ups and downs, and my children have been involved from day one. They have set up chairs, participated in music, helped lead vacation Bible school in the backyard, and delivered meals to hurting church members. The point is that we've shared these experiences, which have shaped us.

This was driven home for me recently as my oldest son and I went on a men's ministry campout. That first night, as the large group of men gathered around the campfire, my son leaned over to me and whispered, "Dad, this is just great!" You see, he had been there in the beginning before any of those men were a part of the church. He had been with me, planning, praying, and serving. This celebration was a celebration for him, and we were able to enjoy it together. That night, I believe he felt a bond that was growing into a brotherhood. I know I did.

It was a powerful moment together, but its importance went beyond nostalgia. It represented a long-term engagement and opened another door for meaningful discipleship. As we enjoyed being together, I knew there'd be other days to speak the truth. But that night I sat by the fire and said, "Yes, son. It is. And you've been a big part of it."

I certainly don't mean to imply that it takes planting a church to truly be with our children. Whatever we do, we can find creative ways to invite them in. Allowing them to share in our experiences and finding ways to share in theirs will offer opportunities to celebrate the journey the Lord has for us all.

Principles of Our Engagement

Some of us may be new to this parenting thing, anticipating a new son or daughter, while others may be feeling like we have missed our chance with our kids. Wherever you are on the spectrum, be encouraged. Don't be overwhelmed. And don't try to over-script things. Simply live life together with your children. And know that it is never too late. Engage with your children. Be with them. Talk about things that matter and share experiences that matter.

Your engagement will look different from mine. It should. We're all different. Remember, though, at this point, we are building principles of practice. We will bring those principles of practice together with some ideas for action, but for now, the following are basic principles of engagement to assist us with the act of engaging with our children:

- Regular—Our engagement should happen consistently.
- Committed—We should be committed to our engagement and follow through with our actions.
- Sacrificial—Our engagement will require a certain death to our selfish desires.

- Structured—Schedule time when your children know they can count on being with you.
- Unstructured—Some of the best times to be with your children come up spontaneously.
- Modeling—Bring your children along with you to do the things you do.

CHAPTER 9

Delight

The Principle of "Taking Delight In"

For I am the LORD your God,
the Holy One of Israel, your Savior.
I give Egypt as your ransom,
Cush and Seba in exchange for you.
Because you are precious in my eyes,
and honored, and I love you,
I give men in return for you,
peoples in exchange for your life.

—Isaiah 43:3–4

As the Father has loved me, so have I loved you.
Abide in my love.

—John 15:9

I have a confession. As I first sat down to write about delighting in our children, I came under a sudden conviction. I was about to talk about enjoying my children rather than actually doing it. It was a Friday afternoon, and my youngest son was due to arrive home from school. It was the first Friday of the school year, and he was already experiencing withdrawal pains from missing the golf course. At that moment I remembered telling him at the beginning of the summer about how we would play golf together on my days off. We played one round.

With this realization, I loaded our clubs in my trunk and drove to the end of our street to wait on the big yellow bus to drop off its precious cargo. A couple of minutes later, my son hopped off the bus and walked over to the driver's side window.

"What's up, Dad?" he asked in his cool, casual manner.

"I thought we'd go play golf," I said.

"We?" he shouted. "Now that makes me happy!" He ran to the other side, jumped in the car with a big grin, and off we went. It was a simple thing. It only took a couple of hours. But it also took intentionality. It required a deposit into my son's life that I almost missed because I was too focused on writing. But in this simple thing, a profound message was communicated. My son knew that I was delighting in him.

Taking Delight In

The word *delight* is complex. It can be used alternatively as a noun or a verb. It can be used in a way that can have many unintended consequences. At times, it can even unintentionally (or intentionally) make one feel as if they are in a performance-based relationship, that is, if they feel pressure to bring delight to another person. On the other hand, it can also be a word and a state of the heart that expresses tremendous grace.

Delight refers to something that gives pleasure when used as a noun. *Delight* when used as a verb means to take pleasure in something or someone. At first glance, it may seem like a mere grammatical nuance. Yet in parenting, as in our relationship with the Father, the difference means everything. *Delight* when used as a noun places the responsibility for pleasure or pleasing on the child. For example, a parent might say to another parent, "My child is a delight."

However, when *delight* is used as a verb, the responsibility for pleasure or taking pleasure in is placed on the parent. In this case, the parent might say to her child, "I delight in you." The child who is the object of delight and knows it will often blossom in the context of a grace-centered relationship with their parents.

Do we characterize our relationships with our children as being marked by gracious delight? I'm not trying to open a wound here, but let's be honest with each other. Maybe there are times when this would be true in our relationships with our children. There are times when I delight in my children. But there are times when I have failed miserably. Often, a different verb would describe my parenting, capturing a different emotion. After all, I get tired. I am selfish. I like peace and quiet. And I don't often respond well to disruptions to my self-centered world. Maybe that's just me. But maybe not.

I suspect we all might struggle with delighting in our children. I also suspect some of us are even wondering how delighting in our children fits into the notion of shepherding our children. Is there a biblical warrant for it, or is it another concept in a long line of child-centered parenting tips? Good question.

Let's go back to our premise. We are learning to parent by watching Jesus as He disciples the disciples. I believe that when we watch the Good Shepherd in action, we will see that one of the marks of His shepherding care was His delighting in the sheep. And I believe if we continue to look, we will see that this delight is rooted in the Father's delight in Him and His chosen people.

The Father Who Delights

First, let's see that our Father loves greatly. Did you know that? I mean, really know it? We might find ourselves speaking of God's love, but what do we mean by it? Often, I mean doctrine of love. I can give an academic defense of His love, but sometimes I miss the outward expression of His love.

Maybe that's why Mark 1:11 speaks to my soul. There at Jesus's baptism, God the Father spoke words of affirmation over His Son. "You are my beloved Son; with you I am well pleased." We are told of God's love elsewhere, but here we hear Him delighting in His Son.

How does this scene speak to your own heart? As a man, it stirs something in me. As I've grown, I've tried to condition myself to not need the affirmation of others to find my worth. Yet, something in me yearns to hear these words from those closest to me. If we are honest, we all would probably say the same.

Jesus knew He was a beloved Son, but in His humanity, it was good for Him to hear from His Father in this way. It was good and right for His Father to speak these words of affirmation over Him. I've come to believe that this is an important scene in Scripture. Mark 1:11 is not a throwaway line. It speaks to the love the Father had for His Son and to His expression of that love as He delighted in His Son. If it was important for Jesus to hear these words, how much more is this true of us?

Praise be to God that He also speaks these words over us! The Father who delights in the Son also delights in us. Did you know this? You need to. In Isaiah 43:4, God Almighty speaks over His children with words of delight.

> Because you are precious in my eyes
> and honored, and I love you,
> I give men in return for you,
> peoples in exchange for your life.

Please do not miss this. In this verse, God Himself is saying those sweetest of words: "I love you."

In Zephaniah 3:17 He doesn't speak. He sings.

> The LORD your God is in your midst,
> a mighty one who will save;
> he will rejoice over you with gladness;
> he will quiet you by his love;
> he will exult over you with loud singing.

God the Father delights in His children in this way with words and song because He claims His own. We spoke of this when we dealt with God's covenants, but His enduring (and endearing) promise is this: "I will be their God, and they shall be my people" (Jeremiah 31:33). It is a promise He made, a promise He honored, and a promise He will see to finality in the new heavens and new earth.

The Son Who Expresses This Delight

God the Father delights in all His children. He delights in His Son, Jesus, and He delights in those who would receive the privilege of adoption as sons and daughters through faith in Jesus and His gospel. Jesus then expressed this delight over the disciples as He prepared them for a life of following Him.

In John 15:9, Jesus describes His love for the disciples as a love that ultimately comes from the Father's love for Him. There He told the disciples, "As the Father has loved me, so have I loved you. Abide in my love." These were words of love that Jesus spoke over the disciples, and they most certainly were words of encouragement. They expressed the strength of Jesus's love for the disciples, but His prayer in John 17 seems to take it up a notch.

In John 17, Jesus is praying for the disciples and for those who would come to faith through their teaching (that is, *us*!). While praying, Jesus says something astounding about this love. In verse 23, He prays for unity, both among the disciples and with the disciples. But He also prays that this unity will speak truth to the world around them so that the world will know God the Father loves them even as He loves Jesus! Jesus is saying that the Father loves Christians with the same love He has for Jesus!

Jesus was consistent and persistent in expressing His love for the disciples. He did this with words, and He did it with actions. Throughout the gospel accounts, we read of Jesus being with the disciples, feeding them, washing their feet, teaching them, and doing ministry with them. He didn't separate Himself from this rowdy bunch of men, and if you've ever sat around a campfire with a group of men, you know they had to have a good laugh together. Jesus spoke of His love for the disciples, and He showed it to them with His actions.

To speak of Jesus's love is probably not a groundbreaking thought for you. But you may be asking at this point why we're referring to the principle of delight rather than the principle of love. When I use the word *delight* in this context, I am trying to capture the notion of love, but I am also trying to express something of the way we communicate this love. To delight in someone not only means that you love them. It also means that you enjoy them. God the Father enjoys His children. God the Son enjoyed the disciples. And we as parents are called to enjoy our children, communicating our love for them in such a way that they know we enjoy them.

Living as the Object of Delight

Maybe you haven't thought about this concept of *delight* in biblical terms when it comes to your parenting, but you can probably relate to its impact. Think about it. How does it feel when someone you know and respect delights in you? How do you respond to this kind of delight? For most of us, this kind of delight is like spring rain causing the flowers to bloom. It brings life.

My parents had their faults (as do I), but they modeled this delight well. For some of you, your parents did as well. For others, you were made to feel like a burden. For some of us, it's difficult to express delight in our children because it wasn't expressed to us. If that was your experience, let me share a story of delight from someone other than a parent to illustrate the point.

The middle school years can be difficult for many of us. By comparison, I seemed to breeze through my middle school years. Yet, in my family there were difficult times. Those were years of divorce and remarriage for my parents. During those years, we moved off the family farm. And during those years I came to know Coach Hillary Carr.

As a middle schooler, I was an undersized kid and a mediocre athlete at best. Yet, regardless of my contribution to the football team, Coach Carr took an interest in me. He pushed me a little harder. He encouraged me. He found ways for me to work with him after school. I was able to help him and his wife with concessions in the off-season. He invested in me during a time when I needed someone to invest in me.

Now, Coach Carr was not someone who gushed with emotion. He wasn't a cheerleader type. But as a middle school kid, I knew he delighted in me. Oh, I don't know that I would have used that word at the time, but I knew he cared. And the impact was deep. I can look back and see his walk. I can see his old blue truck, and I'm instantly taken back.

Maybe the greatest illustration of Coach Carr's impact on me was the fact that as an eighth grader, I joined the wrestling team. After all, he was the coach. Now my contribution to the wrestling team was even less than my contribution to the football team, but he continued to encourage me. He continued to invest in me. And I gave everything I had for him. Looking back on those days now, I am even more thankful for a coach who would delight in me, particularly when I didn't have much to offer him.

Some of us have been "delighted in" in this way. Maybe it was our parents. Maybe it was a teacher or a pastor. On the other hand, some of us were shunned. And our experience can influence the way we delight in our children. As we consider our children and how we delight in them, we need to go beyond our personal history and go back to the Father who delights even when we don't have much to offer.

Delighting in Our Children

Let me ask you to think back over the conversations you've had with your children over the past month. Were you present in those conversations or were you barking orders? Did you take the time to listen to your child's heart? Have you pursued your child to let them know they are worth pursuing?

Please know that as I ask these questions, I am not trying to add guilt and shame to our growing list of parenting failures. I am heartbroken over the growing list of failures in my own parenting. That is why we spent time in the gospel first. I preach the grace of the Lord Jesus Christ, but I must remind myself sometimes. As we deal with these questions, please remind yourself. Know that you have been delighted in by the Father, who sent His Son to purchase your pardon and to welcome you into His family. Know this, and parent out of the overflow of His love rather than in response to your guilt.

But we do ask the questions because they give us a glimpse into what we are communicating to our children. I also ask the questions because they speak to what we mean when we speak of "delighting in." To delight in our children does not merely mean to delight in what they do. It means to delight in them. Are you aware of the difference?

To delight in what our children are doing is to brag on their accomplishments. That's not necessarily a bad thing, but it can't be the only thing. If it is, the message is communicated to your children that they have worth if they perform. Alternatively, to delight in them is to delight in their person, to take an interest in their interests, to pursue their hearts. It is to enjoy their presence and not merely when their presence is convenient for you.

I go back to that Friday afternoon golf game. You must understand something. I love Fridays. As a pastor, I take Friday off. On Fridays, I have a routine that largely revolves around what I want to do. Now, let's magnify things a bit. The Friday afternoon in question was the first Friday of the school year. As much as I love my children, I had looked forward to that Friday to have a little quiet time.

But by the time the afternoon rolled around, I had already enjoyed hours of quiet recharging. The struggle I experienced was an internal struggle with my selfish desires. We all have them. They show up in subtle ways. But often, those subtle ways communicate volumes to our children. Alternatively, our investment in the lives of our children also speaks volumes. When our children know they are loved and, even more, that they are enjoyed, it is like adding fertilizer to already rich soil. The flower is going to blossom.

What *Delight* Doesn't Mean

At this point, I need to offer a cautionary warning. After all, I've used a golf game as an illustration of delighting in my child. To a certain extent, our culture has gone too far in this direction and has perverted the concept of delighting in our children. In doing so, some have created an alternative universe where life revolves around our children. This is not at all what I mean.

In John 17 as Jesus prayed for the disciples, His prayer largely consisted of inviting them into a relationship that was bigger than they were, one that had existed for all eternity within the Trinity. He was saying, "You are beloved, but the world doesn't revolve around you." Our children need to hear the same.

To delight in our children does not mean to build our lives around them. It does not mean denying them the privilege of discipline. The story of King David's passing provides a helpful illustration in this regard. In 1 Kings 1, King David is nearing death. He had declared that Solomon would succeed him as king, but one of David's other sons, Adonijah, is attempting to declare himself king instead. We read of this in verses 5 and 6 where we also see a sad commentary on David's parenting: "Now Adonijah the son of Haggith exalted himself, saying, 'I will be king.' And he prepared for himself chariots and horsemen, and fifty men to run before him. His father had never at any time displeased him by asking, 'Why have you done thus and so?' He was also a very handsome man, and he was born next after Absalom."

King David spoiled his son. He never challenged his son. He never displeased him. As a result, this spoiled child attempted to steal away the throne and was eventually put to death.

Likely, our parental failures will not lead to such dramatic and tragic results, but the warning should not go unheeded.

To delight in our children is to express our love and enjoyment of our children. We are still delighting in our children when we discipline them. In fact, we discipline them because we delight in them, seeking the best for them over the long run, pointing them to the Savior who has loved them at the cost of His life.

Blessed Is the Man

I remember and cherish the days when my three children were born. As I think about those days, I'm reminded of the epic scene when Payne Stewart defeated Phil Mickelson in the 1999 US Open at Pinehurst. Stewart sank a fifteen-foot putt on the eighteenth green to defeat Mickelson and immediately pumped his fist, kicked his leg, and yelled out like a little kid. Today at Pinehurst there is a statue memorializing the celebration. It was just one of those moments in sports, but in my mind, the most beautiful part of the whole scene was what came next.

Mickelson was literally on the eve of becoming a father. His wife, Amy, would go on to give birth to their daughter the following day. Knowing all of this, Payne Stewart walked up to the younger Mickelson, cupped his hands over his face, and said, "Good luck with the baby. There's nothing like being a father!"[5]

The man who had just won the US Open said it best. There's nothing like being a father. I knew it that first day, and I still know it. Psalm 127:3–5 captures this blessing:

---

[5] Associated Press, "Clutch Putts Give Stewart His Second Open," ESPN, October 25, 1999, https://www.espn.com/golfonline/usopen99/news/1999/990620/00001481.html.

Behold, children are a heritage from the LORD,
the fruit of the womb a reward.
Like arrows in the hand of a warrior
are the children of one's youth.
Blessed is the man
who fills his quiver with them!
He shall not be put to shame
when he speaks with his enemies in the gate.

Well said! There is nothing like being a father . . . or like being a mother. Children are a blessing from the Lord, so enjoy them by delighting in them.

Principles of Delight

Again, my purpose is not to give you a formula to follow. Instead, I am trying to lay out principles of practice to guide you in your unique family situation. As you think about delighting in your children, these basic principles may be helpful for you:

- **Enjoy what they enjoy.** Find ways to enjoy what they enjoy. Shared experiences communicate much as they draw our hearts together over a lifetime. As you consider those experiences to pursue your children's desires, understand that those desires reflect their gifting from the Lord.
- **Claim them.** Let your children know that you delight in them by claiming them as your own, both privately and publicly. Words have power. As you probably know from your childhood, parents far too often speak negatively of their children in public. Let others

know that you believe in your children. Your children will find strength in this knowledge.

- **It's never too late.** For many of us, these principles may remind us of our failures. Please know that it is never too late—even with adult children—to begin delighting in them.

CHAPTER 10

Shape

The Principle of "Partnering with the Holy Spirit"

Hear, O Israel: The LORD our God, the LORD is one. You shall love the LORD your God with all your heart and with all your soul and with all your might. And these words that I command you today shall be on your heart. You shall teach them diligently to your children, and shall talk of them when you sit in your house, and when you walk by the way, and when you lie down, and when you rise. You shall bind them as a sign on your hand, and they shall be as frontlets between your eyes. You shall write them on the doorposts of your house and on your gates.

—Deuteronomy 6:4–9

109

My dog Lucy is well trained. Sort of. The truth is that the wellness of her training depends on what you mean by *training*. She knows the commands. She knows what they mean. She can execute them precisely. She knows what you want her to do. If by training you mean "knowledge of," well then, Lucy is well trained.

But there is oftentimes a disconnect when it comes to Lucy's obedience. She simply won't do what she knows how to do. I have, however, noticed a striking correlation. When I have a dog biscuit in my hand, Lucy's obedience is near perfect. But when the dog biscuit is absent from the equation, her performance record is much more lackluster. After many observances, my highly astute mind has come to this profound conclusion: Lucy knows how to obey, and Lucy will obey when obedience serves her true love—food.

Maybe by this time you, too, have come to a profound conclusion. This is not a book about training pets. My dog Lucy is merely a helpful illustration for parenting. As parents we are prayerfully raising Christ followers or rather Christ lovers. Regardless of your vocation, this is your highest and greatest calling: to shape the hearts of your children for Jesus.

Jesus's Shaping Ministry

Before we speak to specifics of what and how we are shaping, let's take a moment to be reminded of why we shape. We're learning from Jesus, taking cues from His disciple-making journey because we believe the church is a biblical model for the family.

Why did Jesus call the disciples? I suppose there are several answers to that question, but at its core, He was preparing them for the work of establishing His church. Now that's a big job. We're talking about evangelizing the world and establishing local manifestations of the church in local communities. We're talking about the daily aspect of shepherding God's people and raising future leaders who will raise future leaders. It sounds impossible, and from a man-centered perspective, it is. But this was and is a supernatural endeavor. Even so, Jesus called to Himself twelve disciples who would execute the plan.

With such a grand vision and seemingly limited resources, it is beautifully profound when you look at the simple way Jesus prepared these men. We've already seen how He spent time with them and enjoyed them, which are beautiful concepts in themselves. But in doing these things, He also shaped them. While He was much more than this, He was still their coach.

Shaping Is Coaching

I just love coaches. The best of them have their players' best interests at heart. The best of them are teachers, but they are more than teachers. They are shapers. Their shaping consists of teaching, modeling, giving tasks, and then providing feedback, all the while helping their protégés excel in their given endeavors.

As a receiver during college, I loved to catch the football. Though often my job was to block other players, blocking in the open field can be difficult. So I needed coaching. My coach taught me the plays and the concepts. He taught me why I needed to block the defensive back. Then he showed me how by modeling the technique. After he modeled it for me, he sent me to do the job. Finally, he gave me feedback on the job I had done.

Do you see that coaching is much more than giving instructions? This was true of Jesus as well. He did much more than teach the disciples. He coached them. Do you see what an essential part of shepherding this is and how we are to do the same thing with our children? I hope so, but there is more to shaping than teaching, modeling, giving tasks, and then offering feedback. Let's talk it through, but first, we need to deal with an important topic: the difference between shaping and changing.

Shaping vs. Changing

Our culture has bought into and propagates the narrative that we should accept our children as they are and never try to change them. This cultural narrative tells us that the best way to show our love to our children is to accept them as they are. On the surface, this concept of shaping our children flies in the face of that narrative, directly opposing it. But that's on the surface, and we don't parent on the surface. This model of shaping our children doesn't contradict the cultural narrative. It redeems it.

As we consider shaping our children, I'd like to point out the obvious. I am using the word *shaping* rather than the word *changing*. There is no doubt that the Christian life depends upon a radical change of heart, which is what we speak of when we speak of the new birth. That change is supernatural. We pray for it in our children but cannot bring it about. The Holy Spirit must do that.

We are talking about our children's gifts, desires, and talents here. Strictly speaking, we also can't change this makeup. We shouldn't change this. Their gifting is given to them by God. Our job is to help them explore and realize their God-given gifts, desires, and talents and then to instill in our children a gospel vision for putting their gifts, passions, and talents to use.

Part of this is helping them differentiate between their idolatrous desires and God-given gifting. Sin patterns are sin patterns, and they must be rooted out. But there are more times than we probably appreciate when the nuance comes into play. For example, if a child makes a lower-than-expected grade in a particular class, is it the result of sinful laziness? Or is it the result of their specific academic bent toward one subject area over another and thus an indicator of gifting? Knowing the difference is why we, as the parents, are the parents. It is part of our God-given blessing and opportunity to learn and shepherd our children.

Another example comes from their desires. One of our sons loves music. He always has. When he was a toddler, my wife and I probably had more significant influence over the genres of music he enjoyed, but that influence has decreased over the years. As a teenager, he preferred music that often gave me headaches. There were times, however, when it was not merely the volume and rhythm of the music that was causing problems. As parents, we've had to engage in our son's music preferences, shaping them by discussing the lyrics, story lines, and worldview his music preferences promoted.

In doing so, we weren't trying to force our son to only listen to specific genres of music. Instead, we were shaping how he looked at music and life through a biblical worldview.

It's an ongoing conversation, but more and more, we see our son making wise decisions while still listening to styles of music we don't typically enjoy. Through it all, our son still loves music and uses his love and gifting to serve the church as a drummer.

In making this differentiation, we are trying to nurture our children by pulling out their true gifting. This is not changing. It is shaping. As parents, we will be called to shape our children's creative or noncreative bent, relational styles, academic direction, and yes, even behavior patterns. God created them uniquely. He has given them to us to shepherd and to shape.

Shaping Their Loves

Like my dog Lucy, our children will follow their true love. We know this to be true because our love drives our behavior, whether those loves are food, leisure, acclaim, or Jesus. I believe that is why, in the context of law obedience, Moses tells the people of Israel that the greatest commandment is that they "love the LORD your God with all your heart and with all your soul and with all your might" (Deuteronomy 6:5).

We are all obedient to our true affection. This truth must shape our parenting. It certainly was central to Jesus's disciple-making process as He shaped the disciples' loves. Two stories (among many other examples) illustrate how Jesus did this with His disciples as He shaped their loves by shaping their worship and celebration.

In Matthew 18:1, the disciples came to Jesus to ask Him who was the greatest in the kingdom of heaven. Establishing a proper pecking order had been an ongoing concern for the disciples. They argued about which one of them was the greatest and even took the argument to Jesus. Maybe they were also including various other prophets and teachers in the conversation, but the gospel accounts are full of examples of the disciples seeking personal acclaim. They worshipped at the altar of self and wanted Jesus to affirm them.

Instead, Jesus redirected their worship, putting before them a child as the greatest in the kingdom of heaven. After all they had accomplished in their ministry with Jesus, this must have stung their pride. Or at least it would've hurt mine. On the one hand, Jesus was telling them to humble themselves. But more fundamentally, He was shaping their worship away from self and to the One worthy of worship, the Lord God. He was shaping their true love by shaping their worship.

A second example comes in Luke 10 when Jesus shaped their celebration. Earlier we said that discipleship is a relationship before it is an activity. But it is also an activity, so in Luke 10, Jesus coached the seventy-two (an extended group of disciples) and then sent them out to do ministry. Upon their successful return in verse 17, the seventy-two began celebrating that the demons were subject to them in Jesus's name. By Jesus's response to them, it is evident that the focus of their celebration was their victory over the demons.

Therefore, Jesus took the opportunity to speak into their celebration. Notice that He affirmed the good work they did, but He also tenderly redirected them. The true celebration was not that they had power over the demons but that they were children of God whose names are written in heaven. The work was good, but the reality of their eternal relationship with Jesus was primary. Jesus was shaping their hearts so their ministry behaviors would merely be an outpouring of their love relationship with Him.

This is our greatest calling as parents: to shape our children's hearts for a true love relationship with Jesus. But practically speaking, how do we shape their love? First and foremost, we pray. We'll talk more in the next chapter about prayer, so I'll save that discussion for later. For now, though, I'll simply say that prayer is the foundation for all we do in parenting. We are to pray as if we mean it and pray as if we believe in it.

Beyond prayer, we shape our children's love by modeling it in our own lives. What do we love? Is a quiet time in the Word of God something we speak of or something we cherish? Do we as parents need time with the Father like we need air? If so, our children will sense it. They won't require us to tell them about it. They will just know. They will learn more from what we truly love than what we speak of.

I've come to believe there are no how-to formulas for shaping our children's love. On the one hand, as parents, we must live within an authentic posture of prayer, marked by humility and dependence. On the other hand, we must take an honest look at our true loves and be willing to repent when we see those loves taking us away from intimacy with the Father. Our children will see this in our lives. They know the difference between what is taught and what is lived.

Shaping Their Behavior

We've said and repeated for effect that discipleship is a relationship before it is an activity. Yet, it is still very much activity. And our parenting at its core is discipleship modeled after Jesus. Jesus shaped the hearts of His disciples, and then He went about the work of shaping their behavior as a reflection of their embrace of the gospel.

After being with them and teaching them, He sent them out to do ministry. In Mark 6:7–13, Jesus sent the disciples out. After coaching them for a time, there was a time to have them test what they had learned. He gave them responsibility/authority and sent them out to exercise it. It was His way of shaping their behavior in accordance with the teaching He had given them. Then He brought them back so that He might continue caring for them.

Jesus was preparing these men for the mission of establishing the church, and He had three years to do it. We are preparing our children for a lifetime of following Christ and productive living. While we will always be parents, we have about eighteen years to fulfill this role practically. That knowledge should relieve us from the pressure to do it all in a moment. Remember, we are constructing a photo mosaic, one tiny photo at a time. It should also remind us that our shaping ministry will look different when our children are three and five and ten and seventeen.

For the three-year-old, playtime with friends becomes an excellent shaping opportunity, as it provides a window into their hearts. How do our children interact with other little children? What does their behavior indicate about whom they love the most? We know the answer. They love themselves more than any other child. As sweet and cute as they are at age three, they need Jesus. But we can relax, remembering the promises of God. Remember, we are only working with a small portion of the overall picture. We can encourage them to think of others. Encourage them to share.

Speak into their selfish tantrums. And when we do these things, we must remember we are doing so much more than trying to adjust their behavior so that they don't embarrass us. We are pointing them to another focus primarily intended to point them to Jesus.

As our children grow older, we continue to shape them through their time with peers, but we are also concerned with how they approach adults. Again, this is much bigger than trying to keep our kids from embarrassing us. Teaching our children how to appropriately interact with adults has a profound heart-shaping effect. One small illustration is teaching our children how to shake hands with a grown-up.

What do you do when you shake hands with someone? You acknowledge them. You greet them. You connect with them. For our children, these are all important lessons to learn. Simply teaching our children how to shake hands with an adult can lead them to respect the authority of their elders while at the same time not being afraid of their elders.

I practiced this with my young children. I taught them to give a firm handshake, look the other person in the eye, and speak respectfully in greeting them. At the time, I didn't understand all that was taking place. I didn't want them to embarrass me by ignoring the adults in the room. I didn't understand at the time but have since come to see that those lessons were important in shaping their hearts toward a healthy understanding of authority. Ultimately, it helped shape their sense of identity and confidence in the knowledge that they had worth as a boy or girl created in the image of God. It helped teach them social skills, forming a foundation for learning to love their neighbor.

Now I didn't understand all of that at the time. But I've come to see that behavior shaping can lead to heart shaping, just as heart shaping can lead to behavior shaping. Our job as parents is to speak into their hearts at the proper time to complete the lesson. Our job as parents is also to know when that is.

As our children grow older, work becomes a shaping opportunity. A ten-year-old is fully capable of learning to mow the yard. That doesn't mean they should do it alone, which is part of the joy of shaping. Remember, shaping takes place in the context of engaging and delighting. We can have our children walk with us while mowing, giving them small portions of the yard to cut by themselves. At first, we walk with them. Then, we stand off to the side of the yard. At the end of it all, we celebrate the completion of the work with a drink and snack. Again, engage and delight and consider the heart-shaping impact of these lessons. Work is a good gift from the Lord, and we should take delight in a job well done. We should take delight in completing the job with people we care about. We aren't simply teaching them how to complete a task. We are shaping their hearts for the work the Lord has prepared for them.

Later, teaching our teenagers how to drive and handle money will be essential shaping experiences. As we spend time (much time) coaching our teenagers in how to do these essential tasks, we are shaping their hearts for stewardship. They must learn to be responsible stewards of the family car. They must learn to be responsible stewards of their financial resources, understanding that all that they have ultimately belongs to the Lord. Again, our children will hear these lessons as we teach them. They will embrace these lessons as they see and experience us living them out.

Shaping Grace

Let me close with a word of caution. Shame is not an instrument of change, whether you are shaping your three-year-old's playtime or your teenager's music choices. Shame has no power to change and has no place in the covenant relationship between parent and child.

I began by telling you about my dog Lucy and my attempts to train her, some of which have gone well and some of which have not. I have often reflected on and reacted to those failures by stating that my relationship with Lucy is not grace based. While some animal lovers may take this to an extreme, the truth is that I was probably wrong about my relationship with Lucy.

I've learned that the best dogs obey because they love their masters above all else. And the best dogs know that their masters love them above all else. The master established a relationship with the dog and then trained it in the context of that relationship.

We're all a little like dogs in that respect. We respond well in the context of relationships. Praise be to the Lord that we are given the gift of grace to live in a relationship with our Master. This relationship was present with Jesus and His disciples and existed in a very distinct order. Jesus loved them, then He chose them, then He shaped them. As we learn from Jesus, it is vitally important that we know this order. It is also vitally important that our children know this order. Our shaping is all of grace. Shame has no place. Jesus died to cover shame, both ours and our children's.

As you shape your children's love and their behavior, your relationship with them is vital. But your relationship with them is always meant to point them to Jesus. He is the Savior. And their obedience, productivity, respect for authority, love of others, and tenderness toward the downtrodden will always flow out of their love for Jesus.

Principles for Shaping

- **Focus on the heart.** We all do what we love. Our behavior is a clear indicator of our true love. As we consider shaping our children, we must first and foremost consider how to shape their hearts with love for Jesus.
- **Bring them with you.** One of the most significant shaping tools we have is bringing our children with us as we go about our tasks. Allow them to be with you and give them growing levels of responsibility as they are able.

CHAPTER 11

Pray

The Principle of "Parenting Through Dependence"

Pray without ceasing.

— 1 Thessalonians 5:17

I distinctly remember the beautiful moments when my wife shared the news that we were expecting. With our first child, I was sitting in our living room in the little Atlanta duplex where we were living. For our second, she woke me from sleep on a weekend visit with her parents. Our third was over lunch at Chick-fil-A in Burlington, North Carolina. I distinctly remember the rush of emotion each time. Joy, deep and rich, seemed to collide and blend with the weightiness of responsibility.

Little in life will impact our prayer life quite like parenting. It could be the acute sense of inadequacy we feel. Perhaps it is the fragile nature of young life. Perhaps it is the overwhelming image of a big, evil world. Most likely, it is all these combined with countless other factors. But what is the impact of our prayers? Why do we pray, and what do we pray will come out of our prayers?

During each of my wife's pregnancies, I prayed for her and the baby's health. Quickly, my prayers took on a new object and fervor. In the days and weeks immediately following birth, I prayed for sleep! And slowly, gradually, sleep returned. Just as slowly and progressively, my prayer life began to transform.

I had often heard the phrase *prayer warrior* mentioned in my evangelical Christian background. The phrase conjured images, but it also conjured confusion. As my children grew, I was still confused over the words, but I began to own them myself. Our children struggled mightily with fear and anxiety. Reason held no sway over their four- and five-year-old minds. So I prayed. There were many nights of fierce prayer, battling in a war I didn't understand, but I pleaded with God for protection for all under my umbrella of care.

In those days the concerns were acute. Many days now, they still are. But the content of my prayer life progressed to other matters just as critical. Though I didn't understand all the implications of God's covenant promise to my offspring (and still struggle to grasp the fullness of these beautiful truths), I prayed for their hearts. I prayed for salvation. I prayed and still pray for them to grow in love with Jesus. And as the Lord has continued to answer these prayers, I find myself praying for Him to bear fruit in and through their lives.

I don't know how old your children are. But I'd be willing to bet that, like me, you've experienced a progression in your prayer life, particularly in prayer for your children. For me, that progression has taken a course from self-preservation to soul provision. My progression has not been perfect, and I don't put my experience before you as an example. But I ask you to come along with me so that we can learn more about this foundational principle of parenting practice.

Prayer as a Priority

You can tell a great deal about a person's priorities by looking at their calendar. Regardless of what we say, the appointments we keep reveal the priorities we hold. In Mark 1:35, we find a day in the life of Jesus's ministry. The day began early, before sunrise. And at that early hour when most were still asleep, Jesus made and kept an appointment with His Father. He left for a desolate place, and there He prayed.

It is a brief snapshot from His calendar, but the priority it reveals is one we find repeated throughout the gospel accounts. Jesus had much to do. He was preaching to great crowds. He was healing the sick. He was equipping the disciples. People wanted His attention. He spent His days with people constantly tugging at His clothing. (Sound familiar?) But He never let those activities get in the way of His proper priority of prayer.

Jesus knew the reality of the spiritual realm. He knew the power and love of the Father. He knew the opposition He faced, so as He set about His mission of ushering in the kingdom of God by mentoring and establishing the church through the disciples, He made prayer a priority. For parents, stakes are high and opposition is fierce, but our heavenly Father is more powerful. Let us also prioritize the principle (and practice) of prayer.

Pray for Your Children

In the early days of parenting, much of our prayer life is centered on the simple prayer for sleep. At least, it certainly was for me, and I must believe that was one of the most appropriate prayers I could have prayed! But somewhere down deep, those prayers were for my wife and me. Oh, there were other self-focused prayers. Just wait till the teenage years. But if we believe our prayers are effective and that God uses them to work out His sovereign will (and I do!), then we must be praying for our children.

I hope you are getting this picture by now, but we must constantly look to Jesus and His care for the disciples. Before He called the disciples, Luke 6:12–16 tells us that He prayed all night for them. The passage doesn't record the content of His prayer, but knowing the mission He was calling them to, we can make some assumptions. For one, I believe Jesus was praying for the Father to anoint these men for their calling. I think He was praying for protection, for unity among the disciples, for each of them to grow in Christlikeness through their ministry efforts, and most likely, for the Father's provision for their physical needs. Those are a few educated guesses about what Jesus may have prayed for the disciples. They are undoubtedly appropriate prayers for us to pray for our children. But in Luke 22 we find a more specific prayer that Jesus prayed for Peter. In verses 31–34, Jesus gave Peter a terrifying revelation. Satan had requested to sift Peter "like wheat." In response, Jesus prayed to the Father that He would sustain Peter's faith.

This is spiritual warfare, and the battle lines have been drawn. Jesus and Satan oppose one another in a battle fought over Peter's heart. Make no mistake about it; this is not an even fight. Jesus wins. There will be wounds—wounds which Jesus will continue to heal. But the battle is real. And the battle is just as real for the hearts of your children.

There is no greater joy than parenting our children. But it also takes everything we've got. We will need to fight for their hearts, and there will be days and nights when the fight will get bloody. With that in mind, I want to speak directly to the fathers with the same refrain the Lord gave Joshua. "Be strong and courageous. Do not be frightened, and do not be dismayed, for the LORD your God is with you wherever you go" (Joshua 1:9).

Many a night I have stood vigil over my children's bedrooms, praying against the spiritual forces of evil. Many a day I have prayed for their hearts, that their faith would not fail. There will be many more. Fathers, you are uniquely called to take up this mantle of prayer in spiritual warfare. It is part of our God-given role to work and to keep the hearts of our children, nurturing and cultivating them in faith and protecting them against the wolves who would seek to steal them away.[6]

These have been examples of how to pray for our children, but please see that a deeper truth is evident in Jesus's prayers. It is the truth of His humility. Remember, He was/is the God-man. If anyone could have said, "I've got this!" it would have been Jesus. But rather than simply trusting His wisdom and discipleship techniques, Jesus prayed to the Father.

---

[6] See Richard Phillips, *The Masculine Mandate: God's Calling to Men* (Phillipsburg, NJ: Presbyterian and Reformed Publishing, 2010). In my opinion, this is one of the most helpful presentations of the father's role in parenting as Phillips applies the truths of Genesis 2:15 to every aspect of a man's life.

How about us? Do we share the same humility? Or do we think we need a few principles, and then we've got this? Oh, I hope not. We've already said that parenting exposes our need for prayer like few other callings. God has called us to care for our children's hearts that we might return them to the Father. It is a high and holy calling filled with joy. And it is one we cannot complete without the supernatural guidance and intervening power of God Almighty. Therefore, we include prayer as one of the four foundational principles of practice. It is not merely the final principle. It is the principle that undergirds all others. We do well to avail ourselves of this privilege and pray for our children.

Teach Your Children to Pray

The adage may seem a bit cliché, but it is true. If you give a man a fish, you feed him for a day. If you teach a man to fish, you feed him for a lifetime. Maybe you've thought that one through when it comes to your child's eventual vocation. After all, we're happy to feed our children, but we don't want to be responsible for providing for them well into adulthood. Maybe you are in the process of teaching them to work right now. Have you considered the importance of teaching them to pray?

There should never be a future day when we are not praying for our children. Prayer is the lifeblood of the Christian life. In a beautiful mystery, God has chosen to work through the prayers of His people to bring about His eternal will. And if we genuinely believe this, we will desire to soak our children in prayer. But we will also understand the importance of teaching them to bring their prayers before the throne of grace. It is one of the central ways we shepherd the hearts of our children, preparing them for a lifetime of following Jesus.

This was part of Jesus's discipling focus with the disciples. There are two places in the gospel accounts where we see Jesus teaching the Lord's Prayer. The first comes in Matthew 6 in the context of Jesus's Sermon on the Mount. There He taught a crowd that gathered around Him on the mountain. Later, in Luke 11, we have another account of Jesus teaching the Lord's Prayer. In the Luke 11 account, we are explicitly told that the disciples asked Jesus to teach them to pray. In each case, we find Jesus praying what we've come to know as the Lord's Prayer.

Do you know this prayer? When did you learn it? I'm guessing that you learned it quite young if you grew up in a churchgoing family. Maybe like me you don't remember learning it. But for most of us, learning this prayer meant reciting the words. It's not that reciting the words is a bad thing. Memorization and repetition are essential teaching tools, particularly for young children. Repetitiously reciting the Lord's Prayer shapes our children's behavior. But somewhere along the way, we need to teach them the concepts of prayer.

While the Lord's Prayer is not the only way to do this, it certainly is helpful. To see this, it may be beneficial for us to have a quick prayer lesson ourselves. The Lord's Prayer consists of six petitions which frame the prayer. Understanding these petitions helps us see that Jesus wasn't merely teaching words to repeat; He was teaching a way to pray.

In the first petition, we pray that our Father's name would be hallowed. Our kids may know how to say this, but do you think they know what it means? First, it means that the God who created everything is their Father who loves them. And for His name to be hallowed means that it would be made holy in our hearts and the world. We pray this because He is all glorious and worthy of praise, so we pray that He would receive the honor and glory due to His name. If we think of this petition in terms of one word, we might think of *praise*.

In the second, we are praying that God's kingdom will come. That means we pray that others will come to know, love, and worship God. We pray that the world will gladly obey God's rule in their lives. We pray that the church of Jesus Christ will grow and be advanced. And we pray all those things for our hearts as well. A word to capture this petition might be *kingdom, evangelism*, or *obedience.*

Then in the third petition, we pray that God's will be done. We pray that we and others will come to know and understand God's will as He has revealed it in His Word. We are praying that we and others will grow in our ability and willingness to follow His will. Maybe think of *understanding* or *growth.*

In the fourth provision, we ask God to provide for our needs, whether physical, spiritual, or emotional. We're also asking God to provide for those needs as we come to need them.

Next, we pray for forgiveness, both that we would be able to offer forgiveness and that we would be able to receive forgiveness. We confess our sins against God and pray for His grace in our lives. We are also praying for the ability to love and forgive others graciously. Think *confession* or *grace.*

Finally, we pray for God to protect us against all forms of temptation and spiritual warfare. We pray this petition to our Father who is sovereign over all creation, including the spiritual realm. Think *protection*. And then in our church version of the Lord's Prayer, we appropriately end with a doxology of praise.

Have you thought through those memorized words in this way? Some of us have. For others, this is a new understanding of words we have repeated since childhood. For all, I want to encourage us to think about more than the repeated words when we teach our children to pray.

Depending on their ages, please give them a note card to keep by their bedside. Help them think through the one word that will prompt each portion of their prayers. Keep it age appropriate. A four-year-old may not memorize six petitions in prayer. Maybe for the four-year-olds, they are learning to praise then ask for needs and protection. Do you see how this simple outline trains our children to deal with their needs and fears, trusting in the Father who loves them? It also teaches us. We should be praying for our children, but we should also be shaping them for a life of communion with the Father through prayer.

Pray with Your Children

Children are perceptive, much more so than we give them credit for. We can tell them what is essential, but they will perceive what is important in how we live our lives. For example, we can say to them that their relationship with Jesus is the most critical priority in their life. But if we spend our time, money, energy, and passion on travel sports, they will see what is important and be shaped by it.

Travel sports is another subject for another time, but the point is valid here as well. We can teach them about prayer and how God uses prayer. But if we don't pray—and pray with them—they will perceive our true beliefs. Show them your true priorities by praying with them.

When we pray with our children, we come together before the throne of grace. We are also engaging in and modeling some essential attributes for our children, namely humility. In prayer, we are praising, but we are also asking. And asking requires humility. That is why most men won't ask for directions or help. But when we pray, something beautiful happens. We are humbling ourselves before the Lord, and we are inviting our children into the act. We all need this.

Let's not just talk about prayer. Let's pray for our children by praying with our children. But let's also ask our children to pray for us. This simple, humble act shows them that we, too, need prayer and that their prayers matter. It invites them into an active relationship with the Savior and communicates their true priorities.

A Legacy of Prayer

I want to encourage you in this journey of parenting through prayer by sharing a recent encouragement I received. Not too long ago, I was sitting with one of my sons on the couch. We were enjoying a ball game, and his phone rang. On the other end was a friend who had been experiencing some recent struggles. I tried to continue watching the game, but one ear was focused on my son.

My son encouraged his friend in the struggle by describing how he had been praying for him, and then he prayed. I wanted to burst into tears. It was a little gift from the Lord as He showed me the legacy of prayer.

You see, I know what a mess I've been in my parenting and how, from a human perspective, the many mistakes I've made in parenting could have destroyed my children. But in this brief snapshot, it was as if the Lord was showing me that He was more significant than my mistakes, that the years of prayer with and for my son had been effective, and that my son was now beginning to carry on the priority and practice of prayer.

We all desire this legacy, but I want to encourage us all with an even more remarkable legacy, one worthy of our prayers. In Revelation, we get multiple glimpses of our glorious future worship. Revelation 7:9–12 gives this image:

> After this, I looked, and behold, a great multitude that no one could number, from every nation, from all tribes and peoples and languages, standing before the throne and before the Lamb, clothed in white robes, with palm branches in their hands, and crying out with a loud voice, "Salvation belongs to our God who sits on the throne, and to the Lamb!" And all the angels were standing around the throne and around the elders and the four living creatures, and they fell on their faces before the throne and worshiped God, saying, "Amen! Blessing and glory and wisdom and thanksgiving and honor and power and might be to our God forever and ever! Amen."

When I read these words, I imagine what it will be like to worship in that setting with my children and their children and their children for generations to come. When we engage and delight and shape and pray, this is the legacy we seek to build. I pray the Lord will anoint us all in this high and holy calling, all for His glory!

Principles for Prayer

Prayer is not meant to be formulaic. It is a conversation with the Lord our God. As you bring your dependence to Him conversationally, here are a few practical principles for you to consider in praying for your children.

- **Pray for their hearts.** Details for the day, physical health, and friendships are all worthy prayer requests, but do not neglect to pray for your child's heart. Pray that their hearts would be transformed by grace, protected from evil, and set on Jesus.
- **Pray for their future spouses.** You are not simply praying for the here and now. You are praying for their future. Pray for godly spouses who would complement them in faith and vision for the family.
- **Pray for their children and their children's children.** Our God is a covenant-making, covenant-keeping God who has extended His promises to our offspring. Pray for them with a vision for joining them around the throne of glory in heavenly worship.
- **Journal.** Journal about your prayers for them and share those journal entries with your children, both to encourage and to shape them.

Section 3

Living in the House

Putting It All Together

Look carefully then how you walk, not as unwise
but as wise, making the best use of the time,
because the days are evil.

—Ephesians 5:15–16

At this point let me take a few moments to clarify what we've been doing throughout this book. We have been building a philosophy of parenting. Upon reading this, you may think, "Well, now you tell me!" That's right. I tell you now because the words *philosophy of parenting* sound so heady. It almost seems like we should be wearing tweed jackets, smoking pipes, and sitting around a fireplace. The whole notion of a philosophy might shut some of us down. Some of us are just trying to make it through the day or night.

A philosophy is essentially a way of thinking. God gave us rational minds and the ability to use them. As much as there may be moments when we want someone to provide us with a set of step-by-step instructions for how to raise our children, somewhere down deep, we know that is not appropriate. You know your child better than anyone else, so instead of step-by-step instructions, we've been trying to train you how to think about parenting.

We began with a set of fundamental beliefs. Maybe the fancy (tweed jacket) way of describing those fundamental beliefs would be to call them the presuppositional beliefs behind our parenting. Those beliefs form our heart memory in the gospel. Then founded on those beliefs, we laid out four principles of practice. Looking to Jesus, we outlined four principles to frame the heart of our interaction with our children.

Using the illustration of building a house, these would be the construction techniques used to erect the structure. But the same foundation and construction techniques can be used to build all types of buildings. And that is where your rational mind comes into play.

The parenting philosophy gives us a way to frame our thinking about parenting. As the parent whom God has ordained to parent your child, you are to apply the philosophy in specific ways to your child. We've been trying to establish a fixed philosophy that has much room for a flexible methodology.[7]

So now, in this final section, we will seek to put some practical application to the philosophy we've been building. But first, a word on intentionality.

A Philosophy of Intentionality

How many times as a young parent have you heard older parents tell you some version of "Don't blink! They'll be gone before you know it!" How many times have you smiled and nodded while rolling your eyes from side to side? Alternatively, how many times have you silently wished it were true?

---

[7] Much of my thinking about a philosophy of parenting has been shaped by the philosophy of ministry training I've received from Reformed Theological Seminary, Reformed University Fellowship, and Reformed Youth Ministries. The latter two organizations have beautifully articulated their philosophy of ministry in ways that have informed several generations of youth and college campus ministers.

Well, guess what. It is true! As we begin putting some practical application to this philosophy of parenting we've been building, the main theme we'll keep coming back to is the following: make wise use of the time. To be wise with time is to be purposeful and deliberate with our time. It is to be intentional.

Where in your life are you most deliberate? Where are you most intentional? Most likely, you are most intentional with those things, tasks, or people who are of the utmost importance to you. You are most likely to be wise with your time when it concerns those people with whom you are most invested. Our prayer is that those people are your closest family members.

That is our prayer, but there is one person who tends to compete for our intentionality. No, I'm not talking about Jesus here. He doesn't compete. He demands and is worthy of our highest intentionality. I am talking about the competition that comes from self.

I've come to believe that the single greatest inhibitor to our parenting is not a lack of knowledge. It is not a lack of experience. The single greatest inhibitor to our parenting is our self-focus. Parenting requires that we intentionally engage with, delight in, shape, and pray for our children. These activities, like nothing else, will clash with our idol of self.

Think about your schedule. How much time do you spend away from your family focused on personal hobbies? How much time do you spend emotionally distant from your family because you are mindlessly lost in some form of entertainment? When was the last time you sat down with your child and intentionally pursued their heart in conversation?

To varying degrees, we all struggle with these questions, which is why I've come to see that the most important element of our parenting has nothing to do with skill or technique. It is quite simply our covenantal commitment to be a parent. It is our intentional commitment to make parenting a priority in our lives. All that we've discussed in section 1 (The Foundation—Basics of Belief) and section 2 (The Construction—Principles of Practice) will shape how you work out the details of this priority. So let the Word of God shape you, and then be intentional, both in your planning and your spontaneity.

Intentional Planning

My wife and I have made a few trips to New York City over the years, and through those trips, I've learned something about planning. I don't need to plan every detail of the trip, but I've got to do a little research in advance to make the most of our time together.

The first time we went, we assumed we would make the plan when we arrived. New York has no shortage of restaurants to explore, sights to see, and activities to enjoy. But we quickly found out that this abundance was a problem. We were overloaded with options but had no direction. We had a great time, but we missed much.

Before our next trip, I talked to friends and family members who knew the city. They asked about our budget and our time constraints and then made recommendations. I read the *New York Times*, I checked the weather, and through it all, we put a plan together. With the general plan in place, my wife and I could enjoy one another's company without the constant question, "What do you want to do next?"

Intentional parenting requires planning. As in New York City, the options and activities presented to us in parenting can be overwhelming. If we don't have a vision for where we are going, we will be shut down, either by indecision or exhaustion. An appropriate parenting philosophy should have a destination in mind and a general plan on how to reach the goal.

Intentional Spontaneity

At the same time, a philosophy of intentionality is not meant to be rigid. The plans we made for New York were not etched in stone. We had a few restaurants we wanted to try out. We had a couple of new sights we wanted to explore. But we were open to something new if it caught our eye. Our plan was not our goal. Our goal was to enjoy our time together. The plan was only there to serve the purpose.

In the same way, we've spoken of a fixed philosophy and a flexible methodology. Engage, delight, shape, and pray are not meant to be formulaic. These activities are intended to inform the way you parent, regardless of the specifics of how you apply them. Our intentionality sets the priority, and the priority protects our focus. When we are intentional about our parenting, we are not merely following a preset course of action. We are also building into our parenting a framework for intentional spontaneity. And perhaps it is in this spontaneity that your children will most fully experience the blessing of your engaging, delighting, shaping, and praying.

With this framework of intentionality, I'd like to now give you some thoughts on how to actually be intentional in your parenting. But please know that what follows are merely my thoughts. Let them stir you to creatively consider how you will specifically apply this philosophy of intentional parenting in your own family. I'll offer thoughts on practically engaging with, delighting in, shaping, and praying for your children. Much of what will follow is taken from how we've applied these principles to our family. Some of these thoughts may work for you, while others may not. That's OK. You take this philosophy of parenting and make it your own.

CHAPTER 12

Intentionality in Early Childhood

Committing to the Role

---

*So I exhort the elders among you, as a fellow
elder and a witness of the sufferings of Christ, as
well as a partaker in the glory that is going to be
revealed: shepherd the flock of God that is among
you, exercising oversight, not under compulsion,
but willingly, as God would have you; not for
shameful gain, but eagerly; not domineering over
those in your charge, but being examples to the
flock.*

—1 Peter 5:1–3

Many of us have heard the phrase "It's not rocket science."
We use it to describe many different concepts or tasks, but
I've come to notice something. Those concepts or functions
which we describe as not rocket science are usually tricky.
Someone may tell us that what we are attempting to do is not
rocket science, but the words don't seem to help because we

are really struggling now. It may not be rocket science, but it is hard!

As a parent of young children, it may be helpful to acknowledge both realities simultaneously. Parenting is not rocket science, but it is tough! It doesn't take a graduate degree from MIT, but it will take everything we've got. We don't need an exceptionally high IQ. (Can I have an amen?) What we do need is commitment. As we begin to put these principles into action, be encouraged. And commit.

Putting the Principles into Action

First, let me start with a disclaimer. I'm not a child psychologist or a pediatrician. I don't have advanced training in the stages of childhood development or the root causes and treatments of various child physiological pathologies. These are important topics, and I've gleaned much from other qualified experts, but dealing with those issues and with that specificity is not my goal. I am a husband, a parent, and a pastor and quite often fail in each of those roles. But those roles, those experiences, and the study which has gone into each of them (combined with my multitude of failures) helped shape what we'll discuss below.

And now another preliminary thought that is not so much a disclaimer as it is a tone-setter. We will deal with more specifics on how to engage, delight, shape, and pray when we get to the older children. In early childhood (that is, babies and toddlers), these principles have as much to do with our transition into parenting as they do with how we interact with our children. Let's explore these principles, understanding that we are focused more on you the parent and your heart in parenting.

Engage—I hope you've realized by now that when we speak of engaging, we are talking about more than simply spending time with our kids. We are talking about being present with them. We're talking about interacting with them in the place where they are and pursuing them at the level of the heart. Engaging with our children is to form and enter into an intimate relationship marked by warmth, curiosity, listening, drawing out, and speaking. So how do we do these things with babies and young children?

We start by understanding that to engage is not merely to take on specific tasks. Ultimately, engaging is setting a context for the whole relationship with our children, which begins when they are babies. Engaging in this stage means giving our lives over to them. To engage is to commit to the role of parenting.

I've told you that we are modeling our philosophy of parenting after the leadership roles in the church, so maybe an illustration from church leadership will help. Each year, our church goes through the process of nominating, training, qualifying, electing, and ordaining new elders and deacons. It is a thorough process to prepare men for the work we believe God has called them to do. But as extensive as that training is, I find myself needing to meet with the newly installed elders and deacons every year.

They may realize what's going on and initiate a discussion with me. Other times they're unaware, and I need to initiate. Regardless, most of these well-intentioned, godly men will initially hesitate to engage in their new roles. For some, fear holds them back. They understand the weightiness of their office and don't feel like they have much to offer the flock they've been called to shepherd and serve. For some, it is not fear but a lack of understanding about authority. They don't yet understand that the office carries an authority that God has bestowed in His Word. And then, for some, the issue is their passive nature. Whatever their hesitancy, I will have some version of the same discussion, encouraging them to commit (or even submit) to their role and engage.

Many parents struggle in the same way, mainly for the same reasons. I certainly understand as I wrestled with many of these same issues. I was busy working in a demanding job. I longed for the time when I could more freely golf, fish, or zone out in TV land. Pre-kids, I still had the role of husband, but time was more plentiful for my wife and me. I could enjoy those hobbies without taking away from our relationship (or at least thought I could).

And then this baby came into the picture. He was cute, but he was demanding. He required total commitment, and I wasn't sure I knew how to give it or, at times, even if I wanted to give it. You see, you are not alone in those struggles. This means that what you need most is not training to engage your toddler in heart-level conversation. To engage, you must first submit to the role. Parenting doesn't get the leftovers. It is primary. And our commitment to the calling of parenting in early childhood is what will build the foundation for years of future engagement.

Delight—For some of us, it may seem unnecessary to be urged to delight in our new babies. But that is not the case for others, particularly those who are honest with themselves. Sleep seems like a long-forgotten luxury. Free time is gone. Our life is no longer our own. All of us experience these feelings, which is why in this time of transition to parenthood, we must guard our hearts against bitterness.

Babies and toddlers are adorable, but they also demand our time and attention. In this stage of childhood, we need to nurture a heart of delight in them, even when they can't respond. Perhaps one of the best times for this reminder is while changing diapers.

Changing diapers is one of the leading acts of selflessness, particularly once the child moves to eat solid food! The odors become more pungent, and suddenly our darling infant seems a little less precious. At that moment, we must remind ourselves that delight is not just for the sweet moments. It is for the messy ones too. Delight in our young children during the chaotic moments will do as much to shape our parenting as it will our children.

Shape—Much shaping is taking place in these years, but for those who don't have a PhD in child psychology, it will suffice to say that this shaping is taking place at the subconscious level.

Our delight in them and tender touch will shape their understanding of love and affection. The strength and stability of our home and family life will shape how they begin to think about boundaries and how they understand the difference between right and wrong. The strength and stability of your home and family life, combined with the way you delight in them, will shape your child as they grow to see how vital they are to the family while being shown that the family doesn't revolve around them.

In small but significant ways, this will shape a healthy, respectful view of authority within them. To try to flesh all of this out, let's consider one practical application regarding our family's worship in the local church. In short, we shape our children's hearts and our own by bringing our children with us.

I've seen, at least broadly speaking, two kinds of parents regarding babies and worship attendance. Let's call the first the "shutdown parents." Before I go any further, let me say that I don't want to offend with the label. In some ways, my wife and I had some of these characteristics. The description is meant to help draw out contrast and through the difference to draw out some important points about our parenting.

These parents shut down everything until some point in the future. Worship will have to wait until the baby can handle it, or maybe until the parents can handle it.

Many factors go into shutdown parenting. Maybe it's fear. Some parents are afraid to expose their baby to the elements, whatever those elements may be. Maybe it is because they are overwhelmed. Some parents need a break, and the thought of lugging a stroller and diaper bag to worship is too much to handle. It's easier to stay home, so that is precisely what they do.

Maybe some don't want to be a bother to others. They are afraid the baby might cry, or they might have to get up in the middle of worship and change a diaper or feed the baby. All of that seems like it would annoy others, which is the last thing they want to do.

And then others can't/won't do anything to mess with the all-important sleep/feed schedule. I'll confess, this was my struggle. I can be a bit of a control freak, and with little else in my control during the baby years, I wanted to hang on to the all-important schedule. We guarded it and resisted anything that would get in the way. For a time, our baby controlled the family.

Again, all of this describes the "shutdown parent." But as I said, there is a second kind of parent. They are the "bring 'em along" parents. The bring 'em along parents don't wait until sometime in the future when things are under control so they can return to weekly corporate worship. They don't wait until they can get a babysitter before returning to fellowship within the church's life. They don't wait to go to the grocery store. They "bring 'em along."[8]

Whether they know it or not, these "bring 'em along" parents seem to intuitively understand that though they delight in their child, the family life doesn't revolve around the child. Instead, the child fits into the life of the family. This practical shaping doesn't come in the form of a sit-down teaching moment with the baby (as if that were a thing!). Instead, it is another example of the small thumbprint pictures that form the whole portrait over time. Over time, bringing them along shapes baby and parents to see their places in the family. And again, over time, the baby begins to form a healthy view of authority.

Pray—You don't need me to tell you this, but babies are like spark plugs for your prayer life. Nothing drives us to prayer like desperation, and in our moments of parenting

---

[8] While I believe it is important to maintain the weekly rhythm of corporate worship within the local church even in the earliest days of parenting, I am not speaking to specifics about the child's physical presence in worship versus leaving them in a nursery. The question about a child's presence in worship is a matter of shepherding and should be discussed with your local pastor or elders. Having said that, I do believe it will be important to include children in corporate worship at a much earlier age than is often advocated for in the contemporary church.

honesty, we are desperately aware of our inadequacies. If you are a parent, I assume you are likely praying more now than you once did.

This is good, but let me encourage you to pray for more than a good night's sleep. Yes, pray for the ability to survive the day for you and your baby/toddler. Pray for their physical well-being. Pray for wisdom in all the decisions you find yourself having to make. But also see your prayer life in terms of laying the foundation for future generations.

In John 17, Jesus prayed what we've come to know as the High Priestly Prayer. In that prayer, He prayed for Himself, for the glory of God, and for the disciples to know and enjoy their glorious union in the Godhead. But in John 17:20, He made a profound addition to His prayer list. He prayed for those who would come to faith through the disciples' ministry. He prayed for future generations beyond simply the here and now. He was laying the prayer groundwork for a long-lasting movement of the Spirit—one that reaches you and me!

Do you think in those terms when praying for your baby? Probably not. Most of us are just trying to get them to nap so we can get a few minutes of peace. That is an understandable and appropriate prayer, but it's not all. In these early years, lay a foundation of prayer for your child's future and generations beyond them. Pray for their salvation, friendships, and future spouses and offspring. Pray for fruitfulness in their vocational calling. Pray *big*. It is a necessary outworking of God's covenant promises to families. God works through those prayers, but He also shapes us and our parenting as we pray them.

Investing in Your Marriage

These principles are meant to be examples of how we bring a mindset of intentionality to our parenting in the early childhood years, but there is a more critical area of intentionality we must also address: intentionality in our marriages.[9]

We've already talked about the importance of committing to the role of parenting. As a married couple, each of you is making this transition when it is easy to lose focus on your marriage. You are physically and emotionally exhausted; without intentionality, early childhood can quickly become a time of drifting apart.

This investment will look different for everyone. There is no blueprint for how to accomplish it, and any blueprint we were to put forward would fall into the category of an empty formula. Time is like a precious and rare gem during the early childhood years (and will remain so throughout your parenting). Whatever it looks like for you, set aside time to talk and listen. Maybe it will be the first thirty minutes after the baby goes to bed. Perhaps it will be fifteen minutes before the workday begins.

---

[9] I understand that in writing about marriage in the context of parenting that I am making an assumption. That assumption does not fit everyone. Many who are reading this are likely parenting as singles. Some of you are single parents by choice. Many more are single parents by circumstance. If this is you, I want to encourage you, regardless of circumstance, to seek out the beauty and blessing of the local church. You are not meant to walk this path alone. Allow or even push your local church to join you in the call to parent your child. It is God's design for the diverse gifting within the body to come together as one cohesive whole under the authority of the Head, the Lord Jesus Christ.

Whenever it is, turn off the television, set aside social media, and focus on one another. The minutes are few, but this can be a beautiful time to grow in knowing one another. It is a time to serve and care for each other's needs. Those roles you've fallen into may need revising. Those hobbies you've given your time to may need adjusting. Just as the early childhood years serve as a call to commit to the role of parenting, they also serve as a wake-up call to commit to the part of marriage.

As you invest in your marriage, you make the most eminent investment in your parenting. We've already said that your marriage will be a source of strength and stability for your children as they grow. For some of us, this is a sobering thought. For some, it may bring sadness as they look back on the brokenness of their marriages and the impact on their children. If that is you, please know that it is never too late. Our children will find strength and stability regardless of age as the Lord works for redemption in our marriage. But for that redemption to be authentic, it can't simply be for the good of the children. It must be for the glory of God and the good of our marriage.

We shouldn't hesitate to seek counsel regardless of where we find ourselves in the marriage union. This is how we invest. Seek out older couples who have "been there and done that." We can seek counsel from our pastors or elders. Seek counsel from trained biblical counselors. This counsel is not a sign of failure. Quite the opposite, it is an honest and vulnerable act of strength. Our children will be strengthened through it.

Stay in the Moment

I look back on our early years of parenting with a mixture of fondness and sadness. Those were sweet times when we enjoyed the excitement of new babies and the gift of a growing family. Our pictures capture those moments. But there were other moments off camera: moments of discontentment, moments of looking beyond the moment. Maybe some of us are feeling this now. If so, we're not alone.

It's true throughout our parenting journey, especially in the early years. More than tips on how to train our children, we need training in parenting. That is why we began with the call to commitment. We've spoken about loyalty to the role. Let's end with a commitment to the moment.

The sadness I feel when I look back at those off-camera moments is mainly due to two forms of discontentment. On the one hand, I was always looking to the next stage. If only they would sleep through the night. If only we could get past the constant feeding and napping schedule. If only we could turn the car seat around so my child could see where we were going and possibly stop crying. In all those *if only* instances, I was missing the moment's beauty. And unknowingly, I was missing out on delighting in my child.

The second form of discontentment came in the form of my professional striving. I worked as a corporate and investment banker while our first two children were babies. There were many long hours and late nights. Some weeks I didn't see my kids at all, even when I wasn't traveling. I remember coming home at night, and my wife would be crying. In a feeble attempt to excuse my schedule and console her, I would say, "It will all be worth it on bonus day." The bonuses were good, but it was never worth it.

Eventually, we made changes to prioritize our family. You may or may not need to make some of those changes. As you think about whether changes may or may not need to be made, I want to affirm something. You should know without a doubt that you can glorify God and be a devoted parent while working long hours. But guard your heart against idolatry. Be equally yoked in terms of family priorities and listen to your spouse with a willingness to be persuaded.

Regardless of your struggle, resist the pull toward discontentment and seek to embrace the moment. God, in His wisdom, gave your child to you. Commit to the role, stay in the moment, and trust that the Lord will provide what you need when you need it. Enjoy the moment and stay in it.

CHAPTER 13

Intentionality in Adolescence

Patiently Pursuing the Heart

Keep your heart with all vigilance, for from it flow the springs of life.

—Proverbs 4:23

"Pomp and Circumstance" evokes springtime. We hear the tune, or maybe imagine it in our mind, and we can picture young people marching into an auditorium, clothed in caps and gowns, glowing with anticipation. We're instantly taken back to a late springtime evening when we either participated in or witnessed that consummate rite of passage. At least, that is where most of us go. My heart, instead, goes to a different springtime event—preschool graduation.

That's right. Preschool. The picture in my photo album is one of my favorites. Our oldest son was five. Adorned with a tasseled cap, he was walking down the aisle at the church preschool graduation, smiling his sweet little boy smile.

I was a proud papa. And yet the over-the-top sentimentality of a five-year-old marching along to "Pomp and Circumstance" wasn't lost on me. Perhaps it was the cynical side of me coming out, but at the time, my smile was mixed with a smirk. Quietly, I wondered if this was all too much—shame on me. Overall, the preschool experience taught me a lot.

Maybe it gets a bit overdone in our participation-ribbon culture where the frequency of celebration seems to drown out the significance. Perhaps we've missed the importance of identifying and marking rites of passage, but my son was passing into a new season of life that spring day. I enjoyed the ceremony and indulged in the photo shoot, but I missed the importance.

Some cultures understand this better than others, but these rites of passage mark the journey of a child's progression toward mature adulthood. Children grow, and seasons change. In our better moments, we mark these changing seasons with rites of passage and shepherd our children toward (and through) them. But often, we struggle to keep up. We miss the season because we are trying to make it through the day.

It's OK. We're on this journey together. We've all missed opportunities. That is why we cling to the image of the photo mosaic. We trust that God is at work in our children's hearts and, maybe more importantly, in ours as He builds within us an awareness of how to shepherd our children through change. Intentional parents understand, or more accurately are growing to understand, these seasons of change and their call to patiently pursue their children's hearts along the way.

A Season of Change

Often, just when we feel comfortable in our roles, things suddenly change. It happens in our jobs. We may finally get to know our customer base when the territory changes. It happens in our friendships. We finally find that collection of friends we've longed for, and then one by one, they move away. It happens in our sleep patterns. We finally find a rhythm for the evening and morning, and the baby comes along.

Life is not static. Change is constant. So how do we deal with it? Some of us thrive on change. We view each transition as a fresh opportunity to reinvent ourselves. We're thrilled at the prospect of a new challenge or adventure. Others of us fear change. It shuts us down and sends us to the weighted blanket. You know, the one that holds you tight, protecting you from all that change.

We all deal with change differently, but we do deal with it. We are adults, and though we have different levels of emotional maturity and baggage, we've developed tools to deal with change. We may not feel like they're the right tools, but at the very least, we have some benefit from age and experience. But enough about us. Let's think about the kids.

Adolescence is one long season of rapid change. Think about that. Long seasons of change can be wearisome. Rapid change can be dizzying. Put them together, and you have a recipe for turbulence.

I've already told you that I am not a child psychologist. We're not going to get into the neuroscience and brain chemistry behind these changes. I'm a pastor, and I've come to see that knowing your specific child is crucial. Before we overreact to outward coping mechanisms, we need to pursue our children's hearts by considering the multitude of ways in which they are experiencing change.

Seventh grade hit hard for one of our sons. He had been steady up until that point, even though he had recently experienced an inordinate amount of life change. But during that year, along with the chemical shifts of puberty, he struggled to know how to react. He wasn't sure who he wanted to be or whom he wanted to be with. And his thoughts changed from day to day.

How do you think he dealt with those emotional changes? Like a thirteen-year-old. How do you think I dealt with those emotional changes? Often just like that same thirteen-year-old. His outbursts of anger, moodiness, or just plain pushing the boundaries of authority were all his way of dealing with his changing emotions. I often responded the same way because I wanted peace after a long day of ministering to others. Sigh.

What he needed in those moments was for his father to pursue his heart. He needed to be known. Certainly, he needed discipline. The outward coping mechanisms at times showed up as unacceptable, willful disobedience. But loving discipline pursues the heart and seeks to understand the issue behind the external behavior. Intentional parenting amid changing emotions sees those changing emotions not through anger or fear but through the lens of opportunity.[10]

---

[10] See Paul David Tripp, *Age of Opportunity: A Biblical Guide to Parenting Teens* (Phillipsburg, NJ: Presbyterian and Reformed Publishing, 1997). I've mentioned him before. I ask that you read Paul Tripp. Read as much as you can, particularly *Age of Opportunity*. Tripp's vision for pursuing the heart of our teenagers has done as much to shape my view of parenting as anything I've read. The title says it all. The teenage years are not years to be feared. They are indeed an age of opportunity.

Our adolescent children's desires are changing and will continue to change. The changes can be a desire for a new sport or hobby. Other times the changes are more drastic, and as a parent, we feel like we deserve reimbursement for our investment in whatever desire just changed. We don't say it (most of the time), but we feel it. But why the change? Is it because they're coming to a hard realization of the limitations of their gifting? Is it because they no longer see the desire as "cool"? Is it because a teacher or a friend said something about their desire? Or is it that another desire has captured their imagination?

Your child may not know the answer to those questions. As parents, we are to approach those opportunities with wisdom. And we should remember all that has already been said about our call to *steward* our children's hearts (see chapter 6: Parenting as Stewardship—Pointing to the Rightful Owner). When we see our role as stewards, we are simply trying to help them find their gifting and assist them as they grow into that gifting for the glory of God.

Whether we are using the language of stewarding or shepherding, there is an underlying assumption: intentionality. We described earlier the two ways many of us react to change. Some of us thrive. Some of us retreat. But both are a reaction. Intentionality, however, is proactive. In our parenting, let us consider a third way.

A Third Way: Finding Stability / Embracing Change

How many times have you wished you could take back a reaction? How often have you responded to your child with an over-the-top display of emotion? Mine are legion. And my volatile reactions have yet to go well. In my parenting daydreams, I respond with a simple, calm reassurance. In my parenting daydreams, I am stable. However, in reality, I am often caught off guard and react like a child. How can we find a sense of stability to set a different tone for our children?

We begin by confessing how we've placed our identity (good or bad) in our children's temporal behavior. Our identity is to be found in our union with Christ. The certainty of His identity buffers us from the emotional neediness we place on our children's behavior patterns. But more than that, Jesus shapes our goals and plans for our children. And with a Christ-shaped goal and plan for our parenting, we can look forward intentionally rather than reacting to the past.

Intentional parenting is not scripted, but it is committed. It is not rigid, but it is thoughtful. It is not a series of reactions. It has a goal and a destination in mind. Intentionality and proactive planning offer stability during changing conditions. And a well-planned route gives you the most remarkable ability to remain calm so you can embrace the change that will invariably come.

We have various optional paths that will take us to our destination. Like the GPS on our phones, some paths are speedy, and some are more scenic. You choose based on your needs, desires, and personalities. But go in a direction.

A Framework for Engage, Delight, Shape, Pray

We have been building what we've described as a philosophy of parenting. That philosophy has as its foundation a set of basics of belief. Then, on top of that foundation, we identified our principles of practice. They are construction techniques. We learned the principles of practice from Jesus: engage, delight, shape, and pray. We've tried to describe this philosophy as containing a fixed foundation and principles and a flexible application plan.

How we apply the foundation and principles in our family will differ from how other families do so. Each family is unique, but to stir up thinking, I will offer some thoughts from our family, along with a few qualifying remarks.

First, what you see here is what I'll call a providential accident. We didn't start with this much foresight. Much resulted from doing what I've encouraged you not to do. Much of it was a reaction to what we saw in the culture and our children. We didn't start with a philosophy of parenting in mind. Along the way, the Lord revealed what He had been doing. He had a philosophy of parenting that He showed us as we were ready to receive it. So, this is a blessed, providential accident.

Second, I am not suggesting you follow this script. It is not a script but has turned out to be a loose outline from which we can (and often do) deviate. Let this fuel your creativity. And think it through with your children, seeking their input.

Third, we've learned from many others along the way. One of the constants has been to recapture rites of passage and ceremonies.[11] They mark life transitions and give us a

---

[11] See Robert Lewis, *Raising a Modern-Day Knight: A Father's Role in Guiding His Son to Authentic Manhood* (Carol Stream, IL: Tyndale House, 2007). Among others I've already mentioned, this title was tremendously helpful in this regard. While I don't subscribe to all that was taught in this book, it speaks well to the power of ceremony and calling your child to a life of meaning.

way to celebrate our children without making them objects of worship.

Fourth, the fingerprints of engage, delight, shape, and pray are all over this framework. They inform all of it, even if they are rarely singled out. I encourage you to stick with the principles and authentically blend them for you as a parent. Be creative. Be intentional. Be flexible. And learn from others. Now here are some thoughts on practical applications.

The Power of Trips

When our oldest child was eight, we received the much-anticipated question from our grandparents: "What does he want for his birthday?" Somewhat disillusioned with the number of toys in his bedroom, most of which he never played with, we decided to suggest something different for our son. We responded, "How about a trip?"

For my son's eighth birthday, my father and I took him to Washington, DC, for a few days of guy time. It was a blast! We toured the sights, played cards, ate ice cream, and enjoyed being together. And what I don't think I realized at the time was that being together may have been the highlight of it all. My son came alive as he knew he was delighted in. The trip reinforced his place in the family. It fostered conversation and fun, and maybe even a little teaching. Quite simply, it was a success.

Guess what happened next? When our second and third children turned eight, they took their trips to DC. It became something they eagerly anticipated. Each child had different experiences. However, the benefits were the same. A gift in

Intentionality in Adolescence

the form of a toy could never have replicated this milestone event.

And yet it wasn't the details of the trip that mattered most. It was the shared adventure. We can't always take a trip to some far-off place, nor do we have to. The point is to invest something of ourselves with our children in a shared experience. We can do the same thing by taking our children on a field trip to see one of the sights in our town. These outings are an opportunity to listen to our children's hearts and invest in their interests, regardless of the miles we travel.

Twelve-Year-Old Discipleship [12]

With the teenage years coming upon us, we intentionally set our kids' twelfth year apart as a year of discipleship. We planned it out in advance, bringing them into the planning. As we approached our oldest son's twelfth birthday, this planning included sitting down with our other children to explain that Dad would spend a little more time with their brother over the next year. We explained that each would get their turns, which heightened their anticipation.

The year began with a trip! We learned the power of individual trips when they were eight and returned to doing this. We gave them the time frame, and then the child got to choose their destination. I had probably thought about taking a fishing trip with my oldest son, but he had other ideas. He didn't want to fish. He wanted a city, so we went to Chicago. And it was awesome!

---

[12] This idea very clearly came from others, namely John Eldridge at Ransomed Heart Ministries and Robert Lewis, author of *Raising a Modern-Day Knight*.

We were there for three days and two nights. We caught a Bears preseason game and then a Cubs matinee the next afternoon! We ate Chicago-style pizza and took the architecture boat tour through the city. We had a blast. And that was the purpose. Period. I had much to teach (shape) over the year, but the shaping was meant to be done in the context of relationship (engage and delight). On the trip, we just went and played.

Upon returning, my son and I began going to breakfast every Friday morning. He and I went for a biscuit every Friday before school for a whole year. When we started, I had a list of topics I wanted to cover with him. There were things I wanted to teach, but I quickly realized it was too much. The engaging did as much to shape as any teaching could. Most of our time was spent together as I entered his middle school world.

However, we also spent time in the Word. Each Friday, we took our Bibles and read through the Scriptures. Over that year, we read the first eleven chapters of Genesis (I believe those chapters are foundational in shaping our biblical worldview), the Gospel according to John, and Romans. We read a chapter a week and then talked through highlights. It was more conversational than instructional.

And then, we took time to have some intentional discussions. We talked about sex in the context of a Christian worldview. I tried to make it a natural conversation instead of a forced talk. This was not the first time we had had a conversation about sex. Knowing pornography is prevalent in our society, I'd taken the initiative to warn him about the unhealthy dangers of consuming porn. Twelve is way too late to introduce the discussion of sexuality and pornography, but it was an emphasis in our year of discipleship.

We also talked about life skills. During the year, I set each child up with a stock brokerage account and gave them a small sum of money to invest. We're not talking big dollars here, but it was an attempt to begin shaping their thinking about money, ownership, and investing.

And we spent time talking about their friends, their fears, and their desires. What I probably (wrongly) thought of in the beginning as a teaching time quickly (and rightly) became a relationship time. On the eve of their teenage years, this proved to be a blessing for us all. And it formed a loose pattern for each child. They knew it was coming, anticipated it, and got to shape elements of it on their own, including the trip.

The year concluded with a special thirteenth birthday party. They invited friends, family, and church members, and we asked the guests to speak words or write letters of encouragement to the kids. As best we could, we were trying to usher them through a rite of passage.

Freshman-Year Discipleship

When our oldest was in his twelfth year, we didn't anticipate future years of set-apart discipleship. As parents, we are called to pour into and disciple our children constantly, but in terms of an intentional year, we were just focused on him as a twelve-year-old. However, as the seasons of change continued to come our way, we realized his entrance into high school would prove to be another significant transition. We had seen the blessing of his twelve-year-old year of discipleship and realized the Lord was working through this intentional time. With his first year of high school upon us, it was time to go again.

At the time, our youngest son was turning twelve, so I would have two breakfasts each week. It meant some schedule shuffling, but we decided it was a priority for our family and made it happen. Along with the beginning of high school, we started another year of weekly breakfasts.

For each of our children, I took the opportunity to take them through a discipleship study called the *Gospel-Centered Life for Teens*.[13] It is a workbook study that allowed us to put language into their everyday experience of the gospel. With the boys, we also read *The Masculine Mandate* by Rick Phillips.[14] During a season of life when those around them are trying to define manliness in all sorts of ways, I wanted to give them a helpful, biblical model as a guide. My daughter and I read *Grace for the Good Girl* by Emily Freeman.[15] We knew our daughter, her heart, and her struggles, and we felt that book would speak to her. The point is not the specific book as much as it is to know your child and to guide them through the season of change as an individual.

This was undoubtedly a time of intentional discipleship, but the books weren't primary. Again, the point was to "be with." It was the intersection of engage, delight, and shape,

---

[13] Robert H. Thune and Will Walker, *Gospel-Centered Life for Teens Participant's Guide* (Greensboro, NC: New Growth Press, 2014).

[14] Richard Phillips, *The Masculine Mandate: God's Calling to Men* (Phillipsburg, NJ: Presbyterian and Reformed Publishing, 2010). This is a book I recommend for every Christian man. I recommend it in premarital counseling and to all the men in my church.

[15] Emily P. Freeman, *Grace for the Good Girl: Letting Go of the Try-Hard Life* (Grand Rapids: Revell, 2011).

all soaked in prayer. Those were sweet times to laugh about goofy situations and sometimes to struggle through the hard ones. And the regularity served once again to be a blessing.

Senior-Year Discipleship

Are you sensing a theme by now? Yes, we like to eat together. We like to be together, and I'm confident the intentionality of pursuit has fostered that enjoyment over the years. As my wife and I considered the changes coming for our children as they approached college, we felt the need (and the desire) to set apart their senior year for discipleship. My discipleship goal during that year was more focused on apologetics. As best I could, I wanted to prepare them for challenges that would come their way in college. But the real benefit was sending them off in the context of the relationship.[16]

We didn't anticipate the unique emotional challenges they would face as they expected the change of leaving home. The change hadn't come yet, but it loomed on the horizon. Each child dealt with that anticipation differently, but the year together fostered time to discuss and pray.

Intentional Spontaneity

Now, after all this discussion about structure, I need to offer a word on spontaneity. Weekly breakfasts during different

---

[16] Michael J. Kruger, *Surviving Religion 101: Letters to a Christian Student on Keeping the Faith in College* (Wheaton, IL: Crossway, 2021). Michael Kruger has written this helpful book in the form of a series of letters to his daughter. It would serve as a tremendous resource for this senior-year discipleship.

years of adolescence might come across as overly scheduled and appointment-like. I get it and can even admit to some highly authoritarian tendencies. But the reality was very different. Our engagement was not limited to those scheduled times. On the contrary, the priority of those scheduled times fostered a lifestyle of engaging, delighting, shaping, and praying.

I cherished those times. They were highlights of the week. But our relationship was not relegated to those breakfasts. Hopefully, you know this in your friendships and marriage. Hopefully, you are still cultivating outside bonds, and if you're married, you're dating one another. If not, begin! And if you do, you will know that the more regularly you nurture friendships or date your spouse, the more spontaneous the rest of your relationships will be. The more you prioritize your time together, even on a scheduled basis, the more you know one another and the more intimacy and friendship grow.

The same is true with your children. And this is true, especially during the teenage years when there is more and more competition for their attention. Set apart regular times to be with them, and you will find the irregular times become more robust. Intentional planning leads to intentional spontaneity.

The Rest of the Story

At this point, you may be thinking, "That's a lot of structure!" Looking back on it as I've written it out, the same thought comes to my mind. Oh, wretched scheduler that I am! But then again, the schedule was never the point. It was a means to an end. So, what is that end? Maybe it is (or should be) something bigger than you imagine.

When my wife and I first envisioned these intentional seasons of discipleship, we saw them as ways to guide our children through what we anticipated to be some of the most intense transitions of their adolescence. To an extent, this proved out, but something deeper was happening. The relationship was being cemented.

When I finally let go of my need to control the agenda for our talks, the Lord gave my wife and me the ability to listen. And through our relationship, He gave our children a desire to talk. Please don't misunderstand and think everything is perfect in our family. Far from it. I can still be overly rigid and self-righteous. My wife and I struggle with control. Our sin struggles are ever present, just like every other man, woman, and child living on this side of Eden. But we have noticed a blessed, more profound change through these seasons.

My heart has been drawn to my kids. I adore them. Fallen as they are and wretched as I am, the Lord has used our time together to further knit our hearts. I sought to pray for them and shape their hearts, but the most blessed surprise is that through all the prayer, the Lord has been shaping mine.

Don't get hung up on the schedule. Throw it out if it is not helpful. But keep the intentional pursuit. Ultimately, that is the point of our parenting, to trust in the Holy Spirit's work and to serve as His instrument by pursuing our children's hearts. There is always a more profound heart condition behind their words and actions. Let us not make the external our focus. Let us not settle for temporal peace but instead dig deeper, with long-term wholeness as our goal. And let us trust that the Father is pursuing us both as we pursue our children's hearts.

Navigating the Turns and Enjoying the Scenery

My wife's aunt and uncle have a place down the inland waterway, opposite the coast. It is a beautiful place that combines the beach's feel with a lake house's water activities.

Several summers ago, our family went for a visit and enjoyed our aunt and uncle's gracious hosting. The food and fellowship were great, but maybe the highlight of our time was the boating. We alternated between rough rides tubing behind the boat and leisurely cruises down the inland waterway.

As we traveled down the shoreline, Uncle Ed described how the buoys marked the passageway. They line the deeper section of the channel and serve as a guide for the larger boats that navigate the waterway. Though the shoreline constantly shifts and changes with all obstacles, those buoys guide the boats safely along their way. They serve an efficient purpose, but I noticed a side benefit on our cruise. Freed from worry about dangers lurking underneath the surface, I could enjoy the beauty around me.

In many ways, that is what we do as we parent our adolescent children. We are helping them navigate the turns, exposing the dangers, and keeping them moving toward their destination—a heart fully alive and in love with Jesus. And along the way, we also get to enjoy the beauty.

CHAPTER 14

A Word on Fear

Fearless Parenting

---

*For God gave us a spirit not of fear but of power
and love and self-control.*

—2 Timothy 1:7

---

*Peace I leave with you; my peace I give to you. Not
as the world gives do I give to you. Let not your
hearts be troubled, neither let them be afraid.*

—John 14:27

Let's just lay it out on the table. What are you afraid of?
We all must deal with fear, but for some of us, those fears
grip us. They control our decision-making. They define
our relationships. They hold us back from trusting in and
enjoying our Triune God. This is true in almost every area
of life, but it can be especially prevalent in parenting. And

if we are not careful, our work of shaping will be shaped by fear. Fear-based parenting communicates to our children a distorted view of who God is and how they are to enter His world. We all have some anxiety, so let's acknowledge it to ourselves and, more importantly, our God. In accepting our fears, let's trust that He is at work, not only in our children's lives but in ours.

Fears for Their Safety

The first time I met Dr. Henry Krabbendam was when he picked me up in the middle of the night at Entebbe International Airport in Uganda. After more than twenty-four hours of travel, I was alone, exhausted, and anxious about stepping onto African soil for the first time. With much running through my mind, I walked out of the airport and was relieved to see Dr. K. holding a sign with my name on it. I believe he was in his early eighties at the time, and he told me that he had been to Uganda eighty times. He was a mountain of a man, though by this time, he was slouched over a bit after years of service to the Lord. With his distinctive smile, he welcomed me to the country he loved, ushered me to the van, and drove off into the dark African night.

For years, Dr. Krabbendam had taught college students and made it an annual ritual to bring some of them along on a mission in Uganda. He loved teaching and expanding the students' understanding of God's call on their lives. But these young people also had parents.

I once asked Dr. K. about his interactions with those parents as he prepared to take their children to the other side of the world. Again, he smiled. He said the parents usually asked for assurance of their children's safety. His response was always the same. He promised that their children would be just as secure in the perfect will of God in Uganda as they would be back home. Rather than offering a promise he could not keep, Dr. K. pointed them to the sovereignty of God.

Those parents were asking what many of us would ask. When fear takes over our decision-making process, we ask, "What if?" Then we answer our questions with worst-case scenarios. This is how fear drives us to control and protect. We believe that someone must control the range of outcomes and that someone must be me.

The shepherd and the parent have two main tasks: nurturing and protecting. We are called to wisdom and not folly, which means we evaluate a situation and make the best decision possible with the inputs we've been given. The way of wisdom doesn't take foolish chances. But how often is biblical wisdom giving way to fear?

We live and raise our children in a fallen world. There will always be danger, pain, and heartbreak. Our fears take on many forms, and some of them are justified. So how are we to respond? Jesus responded by sending His disciples out into the world. Ultimately, He would send them out to establish the church. He discipled them, prepared them, then sent them out.

Parenting Through Our Fears

For many of us, our adolescence is the source of our fear. We're trying to protect our children from repeating or having to repeat our past. Maybe it was the hurt we experienced at the hands of others. Perhaps our rebellion led us into seasons of pain and brokenness. Or our rebellion seemed to carry us away from the Lord.

With all these sources of fear swirling around, it's no wonder many of us spend our days and nights hovering over our children, trying to protect them from others or themselves. But rather than protection, our job in parenting is preparation.

The world around us is a frightening place. Temptations abound. Dangers lurk, just like they did when we were young. How do we move from a mindset of protection to preparation? It begins with confession. As parents, are we honest and thoughtful enough to recognize the fear driving our decision-making and then confess it before the Lord? We must learn how, and the learning begins when we talk through these fears with our spouses or godly friends.

The movement that begins with confession matures into intentional parenting when we lean into what we've already learned. Founded on the gospel basics of belief, we trust in the principles of engage, delight, shape, and pray. As we do, we understand we can't protect our children from consequences and pain. Instead, we thank the Lord for giving us the privilege of parenting them through it. And the way we parent in those moments will do much to shape their hearts for Jesus.

God Is at Work

Ultimately, how we deal with our fear in parenting reflects what we believe about God. Is He a distant deity, or is He intimately engaged in His creation? Sometimes what we say is a far cry from what we believe in practice. In other instances, what we say is a true reflection of what we want to believe, so we must keep reminding ourselves.

Foundational to our belief about God, and thus foundational to our view about parenting, is this fundamental truth: God is at work. He is at work in our lives, and He is at work in the lives of our children. We can say this and, at times, believe it. But we will always need reminders. That is why the practice of prayer is vital. As parents, we pray for the Lord to bless, protect, and grow our children and ourselves. We must pray that the Lord will shrink the gap between what we believe about Him and the practical truths about Him that we live by. Pray that we would truly trust that God is at work.

As that gap gradually narrows, fear will slowly lose its grip on us. As we embrace the truth that God is at work, we'll be able to look beyond the immediate moment and parent with a view toward God's long-term shaping care. We will see Him growing our children through their struggles and hurt.

Parents, please know our children will screw up. They will get hurt. And regardless of what we do, we cannot protect them from those hurts. We are not God. God is God. We can't take on their pain or stop it. That would rob them of what the Lord is doing in their lives. Rather than protecting them, let us prepare them. Let us point them to Jesus in their hurt and trust that God is shaping their hearts for Him.

CHAPTER 15

A Word on Sex

Rethinking "The Talk"

---

*So God created man in his own image,
in the image of God he created him;
male and female he created them.*

—Genesis 1:27

---

*Therefore a man shall leave his father and his
mother and hold fast to his wife, and they shall
become one flesh. And the man and his wife were
both naked and were not ashamed.*

—Genesis 2:24–25

For some of us, talking to our kids about sex is enough to cause us to break out into a cold sweat. Maybe we find ourselves looking back on an awkward conversation with our parents. Others find themselves reflecting on the lack of dialogue with their parents. Many of us have not had helpful modeling in this area of parenting. And those of us who have may still feel unequipped for the task. What is this task, and why does it bring so much angst?

Two words loom large in the minds of both parent and child: *the talk*. When we reduce the conversation about sex to these two words, however, we make a series of subconscious statements. By placing the word *the* in front of the word *talk*, we are making a statement of specificity. It's as if we are describing an event as a proper noun: The Talk. That places an unhelpful level of importance on one discussion. Now, with that mindset, we as parents must research, devise our strategy, and ensure we are up to the task.

The pressure we create when we think about The Talk, essentially reducing it to a one-time appointment, runs counter to our whole premise of the photo mosaic. No one moment or discussion will suffice in our parenting, regardless of the subject matter. And this is especially true when it comes to the subject matter of sex.

Then, there is the word *talk*. It implies monologue rather than dialogue. We talk to someone. We converse with someone. In a talk, there is a person who speaks, and then there are people who listen. In a conversation, there is a back-and-forth.

With all of this in mind, can we redeem our phraseology before we go further? Rather than further talk, let's think about a conversation and a long-term discussion. This is fundamental to our intentional, non-anxious parenting.

Identifying the Authority

The internal pressure we build around this topic is one of many difficulties we encounter. A cackle of confusing voices with varying volume levels surrounds us. Some of those voices are directed toward us, and others toward our children. Those voices attempt to define for us what is good and acceptable. If they are confusing for us as parents, consider their impact on our kids. How do we navigate through the noise?

By now, we've established a pattern of answering our questions using the Scriptures. We've sought to do so throughout our time together in this book, seeking to build a living rhythm. The Word of God is our authority on all topics, including this one. That is not to say we can't benefit from other resources, but we must measure their authority in terms of their fidelity to Scripture. For our teenagers, that may seem like an unpractical notion. But as their parents, we are to anchor them in the storm. We serve as an anchor when we remain rooted under the authority of God's Word. We are to stay faithful. And we are to begin early.

Defining the Issue

There was a time (or at least we thought there was) when talking with our kids about sex was an issue of teaching them about God's design for and blessing of the sexual relationship meant to exist between husband and wife. We are no longer left with that assumption.

First, rather than the word *sex*, we often use *sexuality*. This word seems to encompass more. It captures the issues of gender, preference, or orientation. We add pornography and the old-fashioned discussion around fornication and adultery. Our culture assumes a specific authority regarding these matters, which we grant when we become passive by not entering a conversation with our children. So, let's have a conversation.

Two direct passages taken from the first two chapters of the Bible speak volumes about the subjects of sex and sexuality. Genesis 1:27 tells us that God created man and woman in His image. Now granted, we must first recognize the authority of Scripture, but having recognized that authority, we must let it shape our minds. The Bible tells us that God assigns gender. Therefore, if we believe in God, He made us the gender He wanted us to have. And His design and choices for us are not only good—but *very good*.

In Genesis 2:24-25, we see God's wonderful gift of sex to a husband and wife for their enjoyment within the sacred and intimate bond of marriage. Hence, it's specifically between men and women who yoke themselves together through marriage. And don't miss that this gift is a beautiful gift from an abundant God. He's not holding out on us. But the advantage is only good when enjoyed according to His design.

These passages and these truths are simple, but that does not mean everyone accepts them. These truths are under attack by a world that denies the Creator. And with growing frequency, fundamental truths are being dismissed by many who supposedly acknowledge Him. There are professing Christians who waver on the Bible's simple truths. By simple we don't have to be simplistic or naive. But there is beauty in simplicity.

Our calling as parents is to get ahead of the competing voice of culture by initiating a long-term conversation with our children about sex. We are seeking to shape our children's hearts to see God as their authority and to measure other voices against the plumb line that is His Word. But to do so, we must enter and stay in the fight.

Engaging the Issue

This battle begins early. Much earlier than many parents think. We should lay the foundation with children between ages three and five by talking with them about how God created their bodies. In doing so, we are communicating a couple of critical messages. God was thoughtful in making them, and He did all things well. We are preparing them for a world that tells them gender is fluid and is up to their desire.

We are also describing their bodies using appropriate names long before the world perverts or adds shame to those words. This gives us a vocabulary that we will build on as they grow and sets an atmosphere in our family where our children know they can come to us to talk about anything. Our comfortable presence in those conversations (even if faked) will lay a solid foundation for the future.

As our children grow older, we build on the foundation. Their God-designed and God-given body parts are not for others to touch or see. Again, this conversation needs to happen much sooner than many parents think. We're engaging in the battle against pornography, preparing our children for the barrage of images flooding their world.[17] Our engagement begins early and develops gradually as they are better prepared to handle the conversation.

As our children grow into teenagers, the conversations may seem to pick up the pace with shocking speed. By that point,

---

[17] John Perritt, *Not If, But When: Preparing Our Children for Worldly Images* (Ross-shire, Scotland: Christian Focus Publications, 2020). John Perritt has written this helpful book meant to guide the conversation with young children about the appropriateness and inappropriateness of images, laying the early groundwork for a long-term conversation around pornography.

they've already encountered pornography, homosexuality, and the transgender community, not to mention our culture's casual approach to heterosexual activity outside marriage. With these adversaries lurking around every corner, it is easy for us as parents to be overcome by fear. It is tempting to retreat. But retreat is a delay tactic. It doesn't defeat the enemy. We must resist that urge and instead engage, delight, shape, and pray.

How? Many of us still feel ill-equipped. While there may be some truth in that fear, we're armed with many resources. If we are Christian parents, we have the gift of a more prominent covenant family called the church, which means we don't have to go it alone. We can seek the wisdom of pastors, elders, and older parents who have already been there. We can lean on their experience and look to their knowledge for practical guides.[18, 19]

---

[18] Stan Jones and Brenna Jones, ed., God's Design for Sex series (Colorado Springs: NavPress, 2019). Professor and author Stan Jones along with his wife and ministry partner, Brenna, have edited and produced this series of books under the heading God's Design for Sex. Their wisdom and practical help begin early as they initiate the conversation with their first book aimed at children ages three to five years old. The series consists of four books intended to continue the conversation on through the teenage years.

[19] Cooper Pinson, ed., *Alive: Gospel Sexuality for Students* (Greensboro, NC: New Growth Press, 2018). Harvest USA is a ministry that seeks to engage in the lives of those who are sexually broken with the hope of the gospel. The ministry has prepared this helpful study guide with church youth leaders in mind. It is also a great resource for parents of teenagers who desire a guide for applying the gospel to the issues of sex and sexuality.

Hope for Late Starters

Some of us are reading this and are likely thinking, "I'm too late!" Many of us didn't start talking to our three-year-olds about God's good design for their bodies. Some of us have teenagers who are already struggling with pornography, sexual temptation, or sexual activity. Are we too late? No! The best time to begin this conversation for all of us is now.

I remember awkwardly broaching this subject with my twelve-year-old children. I have done little of what I've described to you. I was late. And my attempts to catch up were forced. My children often responded with silence and drooping heads. But we prayed, and we persisted. I don't want to paint a rosy picture, but I like to offer encouragement. Over time, through prayer and gracious persistence, those conversations can become more natural. They can become opportunities for parents and children to experience the grace and forgiveness of Jesus Christ. They can become opportunities for the Lord to strengthen us and rewrite generational stories. You aren't too late. Start now.

CHAPTER 16

A Word on Missional Living

Living for Others

He must increase, but I must decrease.

—John 3:30

Standing beside a riverbank and looking into the peaceful water as it flows by, you might be excused for minimizing the power of the current. The scene seems calm until you try to stand in the river. The force of the flowing water is enough to knock you over, which is why we do our best to canoe downstream. It's why we go with the flow.

But going with the flow is one thing when talking about a lazy summer afternoon on the river. It is something entirely different when we are talking about raising children. That flow may not take us in a helpful direction.

We live in a selfie culture. Sure, the selfies offer lighthearted fun, but those self-portraits have begun to represent a broader societal movement, indicating a more profound inward movement toward self. It seems that everything in our culture is meant to reinforce the power of self-gratification and self-justification. We steer clear of the hard in favor of the easy. We build calendars around our needs, wants, and desires. And the predominant culture of parenting has bought into this hook, line, and sinker.

With this cultural background before us, John the Baptist's words in the Scripture stick out like an oasis in the desert. "He must increase, but I must decrease" (John 3:30). John is saying that his life's purpose is to live for Jesus, to point others to Jesus, to give of himself, and to be inherently *other* focused. John's words and his life were the very pictures of paddling upstream. And if we are to embrace them in our parenting, we will soon discover the power of the current.

The Shaping Power of Missional Living

I'm not sure that was the most encouraging advertisement for missional living, but it is an essential aspect of our ministry as parents. I am sure it is worth the intentional effort because one of the most effective ways we can shape our children's hearts for Jesus is to direct them away from themselves and toward others.

After all, Jesus summarized the essence of biblical gospel living as loving God with everything in you and loving your neighbor as yourself. But what is love? We can talk about love at length, even trying to define it across pages of text. On some level, that can be helpful, but I've come to believe the essence of love can be summarized this way: complete *other* focus. It is living with a heartfelt concern for another person (or other people) with our attention, intentions, and actions focused outward on them, not on ourselves.

Now that is countercultural love! So how do we do it? There is no magic formula. But I want to encourage us to set a culture in our families of missional living. This missional living can take many forms, but in all its states, it is *other* focused.

A culture of missional living is not merely going on a short-term mission trip as an isolated experience, separate and distinct from our everyday existence. Please don't get me wrong. There are many good reasons to take short-term mission trips, and some bad ones.

Far too often, I have heard people come back from short-term mission trips and give their report, maybe at a church gathering, maybe over coffee with a friend. What do we often hear when the trip is to a poverty-stricken location? Usually, these trips take people out of their comfort zone and into a setting where for the first time, they encounter abject poverty. Often in these situations, the report goes like this: "I was amazed at how poor the people were and how little they had. It made me so thankful for how God has blessed me!"

Thankfulness is good, and often our children need a heavy dose of perspective. But thankfulness for my material blessings is still a me-focused outcome of short-term missions. What if, instead of this new-perspective-on-my-blessings approach, we took a different approach to those short mission experiences? What if we approached them with a focus on sacrificial service, loving evangelism, and long-term relationship building? That would require something of our hearts. It would require getting outside of self. It would require the work of the Holy Spirit appropriated through intentional prayer. But oh, the fruit!

Now think about it. What we've just described sounds like more than the typical short-term mission trip, doesn't it? It sounds more like missional living. It sounds like a way of thinking, living, and loving that is not relegated to a week in the summer but to the entirety of life. How do we build this into the hearts of our children? How do we craft this into the identity of our families?

We've got to go back to the photo mosaic. We're not painting the portrait in one sitting. We're intentionally shaping their hearts (and *our* hearts) over a thousand little moments. And those moments come together to shape the whole.

It starts when we stop protecting our children from "the hard." Life in this fallen world can be challenging. Loving others who are different from us can be hard. And we don't like hard. Neither do our children, but more and more, our culture is telling parents to protect children from "the hard."

I get it, and the best examples of this in my family have come about against my wishes. When our children were eleven, nine, and seven, the Lord called our family to move to a new city to plant a church. They would have to leave family, friends, school, and comfort to start all over. My wife and I would never have intentionally chosen that "hard" for our children. Honestly, we weren't sure we wanted to choose it for ourselves. We would have preferred to protect them instead and, in many ways, we tried.

But the "wisdom of the world [and of me] is folly with God" (1 Corinthians 3:19). The wisdom of God is shown on the cross. We cannot bear the cross of Christ, but we are called to take up our cross to love God by serving others. The Lord brought about "hard" for our children; through the years, we've seen the beauty He has borne out of it. The very thing we would have protected them from is what He has used to bless and shape them.

How often do we, as parents, in big and small ways attempt to circumvent the work of the Spirit by ducking and dodging His work of pruning? And yet His ways are perfect. As parents, let us set a culture within our families of joyful, other-focused, missional living that does not run from "the hard."

It is not embracing "the hard" that shapes our children's hearts for Jesus. It is understanding and celebrating why. It is engaging in our children's lives and delighting in them as we draw them out of self-focus and into focusing on others. It is celebrating the work of Jesus in our own lives that allows us to love others well. This celebration of gospel transformation in our families is deeply rooted in prayer and profoundly impacts parents and children. Let us celebrate with our children how the Lord blesses them and others through missional living.

This type of other-focused love is and will be distinct. It will mark our families as different and sometimes make us feel as if we are paddling upstream. But it will be beautiful. So let me paint a picture for you of this beauty. Imagine the joy of seeing your teenager choose to befriend another kid not because they will advance your child's social popularity but because they are made in the image of God and need a friend. Imagine the joy of seeing your adult children choose a church not because that church caters to their needs but because it is marked by loving, intergenerational servanthood. Imagine the joy of knowing your children actively engage in the battle for the hearts of their friends who are desperately struggling against sin.

These are beautiful pictures! These are pictures worthy of our prayers. And these pictures are painted over the years, through a thousand little, intentional moments. Some of those moments come naturally and easily. Some are hard. All are good. Parents, please persevere in decreasing so that Jesus might increase, both in your life and in the hearts of your children.

CHAPTER 17

A Word on the Transition to Adulthood

Independence Is the Goal

And behold, I am with you always, to the end of the age.

—Matthew 28:20

Early on the morning of my oldest son's fifteenth birthday, we drove to the department of motor vehicles office. It was a day my son had long anticipated because he was eager to get his learner's license. Actually, he was anxious to get his driver's license, and this was the required first step.

That evening he was ready for the second step. As soon as we finished dinner, he wanted to go for his first lesson. I took him to a low-traffic area in the athletic complex close to our home and parked in an empty parking lot. After putting the car in park and turning off the engine, we traded seats and the adventure began.

That first lesson was spent mainly in the parking lot, though we did venture down the street and into another parking lot. We were taking baby steps, but we were moving forward. And then the following evening, we got right back at it. He was anxious to learn because he was anxious to branch out on his own.

Independence is hardwired into the heart of a teenager. And that wiring seemed to pop out everywhere when it came to driving! Even my younger children wanted to sit in on the driving lessons. They were enthralled by the idea of their brother driving on his own and hopefully taking them with him.

How do you handle that desire as a parent? Do you approach it begrudgingly? Do you secretly (or not so secretly) wish they could remain cute (and dependent) toddlers? Do you fight back when they start trying to stretch their wings, particularly when they do so in clunky teenage ways? Or do you see something natural, even God-given, in those desires? Could you learn to work with them, shaping them in preparation for the independence they were created to experience?

The Goal

The transition to adulthood can be a beautiful, even enjoyable transition, both for the child and the parent. We ought to prepare for the transition thoughtfully and intentionally. Some of you are in it now. Some of you are trying to potty train your toddler and can't imagine looking to that far-off horizon. But wherever you are in the parenting journey, it is essential to remember your goal.

For Christian parents, our goal and constant prayer is to shape our children's hearts so they will desire an intimate, life-giving relationship with their Lord Jesus Christ. As we've said, we can't produce this desire in our children, but we can trust in God's covenant promises and then prayerfully shape them for that relationship. And within the context of that goal, our calling is to raise them to be independent, self-sustaining, productive Christ followers.

This independence should be our desire. It is also the movement that is taking place in our adolescent children's hearts. They don't always express this movement in the most helpful ways, but it is their trajectory. And we do well as parents to recognize, embrace, and shape this path.

The Model

Again, Jesus is our model. He drew the disciples to Himself so He might equip them as apostles to establish the church. He intentionally (and intensely) poured into them for a season, but His plan was always to leave. He invested His life into shaping their hearts, minds, and actions, all to prepare them for the work He had called them to do.

This was the goal of His engaging, delighting, shaping, and praying. Every moment prepared them for the moment when He would leave. How about us? Are we preparing our children for independence? Or are we holding on too tightly, resisting the natural transition occurring in their hearts?

This doesn't mean we should not discipline them when those independent desires are expressed in self-centered, sinful ways. We discipline out of love. We discipline to shape. But the shaping is not meant to squash the desire for independence. It is intended to redirect it.

Jesus rebuked James and John when they got too brash and suggested they use their power to call down fire upon the Samaritan village (Luke 9:51–56). But He also sent them out to stretch their ministry wings. And He promised the Helper (John 14:15–31) as an encouragement for when He would eventually leave. In short, He prepared them for what was to come.

What does this preparation for, and even embrace of, independence look like for us as parents? It shows up in hundreds of different ways, all communicating a common message. For example, I recall telling my youngest son to come outside with me to the grill. I only half jokingly said I would do better than I had done with his brother at preparing him to be on his own. I showed him how to light the grill, prepare the meat, and cook it. I told him a man needs to know how to cook with fire!

It was an exaggerated lesson that we had fun with, but it was part of emphasizing a point. "You are going to be on your own. You need to know how to prepare a meal." Oh, and then the other part: "Real men cook with fire!"

It's one small example. But the lessons start much earlier. We teach our children about money and work by using an allowance. We teach them about tithing with those allowances. We teach them about bank accounts and bills. We teach them to look adults in the eyes and shake their hands firmly. We teach them how to write a thank-you letter. We teach them how to speak to someone about a job. These little lessons are unified around a shared vision. "I believe in you. You are capable. I'm launching you out with a set of tools so that you can make it."

But we need also to remember there is a progression to those moments. These independence lessons don't begin at age eighteen. They start much earlier. No, we don't give a ten-year-old the same level of independence as an eighteen-year-old. But at the same time, if we haven't given appropriate levels of responsibility and autonomy to the ten-year-old, they won't be able to handle it at eighteen. Recognize their growing need for independence throughout adolescence rather than being surprised by it and prepare them for it. In this way, we can celebrate their natural growth rather than see it as a source of frustration.

Work Yourself Out of a Job

When I taught my oldest to drive, I'm unsure who was the most excited, him or me. At that point, my wife and I felt a lot like unpaid Uber drivers. Our kids always needed to be somewhere, so we were always driving. That meant the driving lessons allowed me to work myself out of a job. It took an investment of time and intentionality, but it bore sweet fruit when our oldest started driving his younger siblings.

Those were moments I looked forward to and enjoyed. But there was another moment I wasn't prepared for. No one ever told me what it would be like that first time I passed by my son when he was driving on his own. Sure, I would pass other friends while they were driving, but I never thought anything about it. Something was different that first time I passed my son. Suddenly, I saw him in a different light. He was growing up to be a strong young man. He was growing in independence. And it was good and right. The sight caught me off guard, but it was a sweet reminder.

In parenting, we are essentially working ourselves out of a job. Our children must eventually leave and cleave. The command for them to cleave to their husband or wife (Genesis 2:24; Matthew 19:5) means we must let them leave, either as married or single adults. Along the way, we must all let go of different aspects of parenting, but in time we will have to let go. However, if we do it right even though we'll work ourselves out of a job, we won't work ourselves out of a relationship.

When our oldest son (the driver) went to college to make his way into the world, watching was a delight. But before he left, I sat him down and told him that my advice giving was about to change. There would be fewer and fewer occasions when I would initiate the advice, but I would always be there when he needed me. He was at the point, though, when he needed to be the one to initiate. He needed to ask. And advice or no advice, I would be with him every step of the way.

I didn't particularly want to have that talk at the time, but over the long term, I desire a relationship most with my son. It feels like Jesus is communicating some of that to the disciples in Matthew 28:20. By that point, He had been pouring into them. He was now ready to send them out into the world. It was time for them to do the work. He sent them with this encouragement: "And behold, I am with you always, to the end of the age."

The disciples needed that encouragement in their work of establishing the church. You and I need it in our calling as parents. And our children need it as they transition into adulthood.

CHAPTER 18

A Final Word

A Messy Path to a Glorious Destination

But we have this treasure in jars of clay, to show that the surpassing power belongs to God and not to us.

—2 Corinthians 4:7

And I am sure of this, that he who began a good work in you will bring it to completion at the day of Jesus Christ.

—Philippians 1:6

I honestly don't remember the details, but I distinctly remember my counselor's words: "The gospel is messy when worked out in our lives." I believe we were talking about a particular strand of teaching, one that seemed to make the Christian life out to be formulaic, neat, and tidy. It presented

Christian obedience and blessing in a logical flow where everything worked out according to the plan.

My counselor was wise enough to know that I could fall into that thinking. He pointed out the messiness of the gospel in the context of this *other* teaching, but he was also exposing it *in me*. On the one hand, I desired structure and order. On the other hand, in my more honest moments, I feared it. In my more honest moments, I know that I am a mess, my motivations are a mess, my past is a mess, and my daily walk with Jesus is a mess. In my more honest moments, I know that if the Christian life is to be based on a neat set of inputs (by me) and outputs (seemingly secured by me), then I'm in trouble.

After our time together, I fear I've done the same. Please do not hear this as a formulaic process meant to produce good kids. Wherever you are on this God-ordained parenting journey, please know that all we have discussed in this parenting philosophy is to be read and lived out through the lens of grace.

You Will Be Messy

We've talked a lot about pictures. We've even tried to illustrate this journey of parenting in terms of the thousands of little pictures which will help shape the mosaic that is and will be your child's life. On the one hand, that image is meant to be an encouragement. Your parenting does not rest on one single moment. But on the other hand, maybe the thought is terrifying because if you are like me, there are many pictures you would like to delete.

When our family gets together to take a photo, we'll snap what seems like hundreds of individual pictures. Then we'll cull through those to find the one or two where no one is blinking and we're all looking in the same direction with natural, casual smiles. The rest we delete. Don't you sometimes want to do the same?

There are pictures in my past that haunt me. Scenes remain in the photo stream of my mind from when I lost my temper, when I've made decisions based on self-interest, and when I've shut my kids out because I was too tired and just wanted to numb myself in front of the TV. How do these pictures fit into this neat philosophy we've built here? I want to delete them, and I bet you would too.

How much power do those outtakes have? Well, they do count. We can't simply delete them. But they don't have to have the final say. Life is messy. Our parenting is messy. And our growth in Christ is messy. Don't let me or anyone else try to tell you otherwise. But Jesus came for messy people. He came for messy children, and praise the Lord, He came for messy parents. And that tells us that our gracious God can use even those bad photos to paint a glorious portrait.

Often the most effective picture is different from the one where you nailed the landing. Often, the picture that leaves the most lasting impact is the one where you failed, and then in your brokenness, you repented. That is the picture our children need to see. Our children need to know that we need Jesus. And that is what they see when we come to them to confess our anger, our selfishness, our sin. Because in those moments, they see the true foundation for our hope—Jesus.

They Will Be Messy

There are those pictures from our parenting that we would like to delete. But there are also those pictures that capture seasons in our kids' lives that we fear may never end. Again, if we have built a philosophy of parenting that depends on a particular set of our inputs to produce a specific set of outputs, well, we lose the ability to live in the mess.

Hopefully, you are willing to acknowledge that your parenting will be messy. But you also need to know that your children's lives will be messy. They are, after all, our children! Yet, that truth alone may be the root of our fears regarding their messiness.

Often, we fear the mess because of what it might say about us. Have you felt the sting of eyes peering over at your table when your toddler screamed and threw his food on the restaurant floor? Of course you have, unless you've decided to shut yourself in the house for eighteen years! Why did that sting feel so painful? If you are like me, it is because you automatically began assuming what that other person was thinking about your parenting.

We all do this. We build an identity around our children and their behavior. But just because we do it doesn't mean we shouldn't resist it. Like us, our kids are messy, and one of the greatest gifts we can give them is the gift of freedom. No, I don't mean the freedom to pitch a fit. I mean the freedom from their actions being the defining mark in our identity as parents, whether that action is a temper tantrum or a game-winning home run.

Identity is often a significant issue for many parents. Oh, let's be honest; it is an issue for most of us. But there is another fear we bring to the messiness: Does this moment represent the complete and final picture?

There is a saying regarding parenting: "The days are long, but the years are short." During those long days, we can confuse the giant picture mosaic for the individual thumbprint. We can despair, thinking we are stuck in a particular image.

In those moments, let us take a deep breath, lean on the body of Christ, and go back to the basics of belief we spoke of earlier. Reflecting on those foundational truths won't necessarily wipe away all our fears, but it will give us a context for the messiness. We need perspective. We need grounding. And our grounding is to be found in the gospel of Jesus Christ and His covenantal promise to us and our offspring.

The Glorious Destination

On the wall beside my desk is a painting by my favorite artist—my wife! It is a painting of brightly colored jars of clay which sets a tone for all that happens in that office and my life. Those clay jars inspire me because they instill a sense of beauty and creativity. But they also bring meaning.

I asked my wife to paint the jars of clay because I needed a constant reminder. In 2 Corinthians 4:7 the apostle Paul wrote, "But we have this treasure in jars of clay, to show that the surpassing power belongs to God and not to us."

You see, the jars are beautiful, but they are *fragile*. They serve a purpose, but they are *imperfect*. Just like us parents. But lest we despair in our fragility and imperfection, Paul reminds us of the surpassing power that belongs to the

Lord our God. The treasure he speaks of is the powerful and abiding truth of the gospel of Jesus Christ. Most importantly, that treasure's effectiveness and transforming power are not dependent upon our perfection. They are dependent upon our God.

And by the power of God, that treasure will culminate in glory. On the messy days, we parents need the reminder that this is not the end. But also, be reminded that the best days are only mere shadows of what is to come. The Lord has entrusted these children to us. One day, we will return them to Him. And on that day, the messiness will be fully and finally redeemed. We parent with that day in view. But praise the Lord, we are not left to our strength and wisdom!

Parents, remember we are jars of clay, beautiful and fragile. Remember it. But also, never forget that the surpassing power belongs to God. He called us to this work of parenting, and He will see us through. With that hopeful truth before you, parent in His power! Parent by His grace!

And I am sure of this, that he who began a good work in you will bring it to completion at the day of Jesus Christ

—Philippians 1:6

Soli Deo gloria!
To God alone be the glory!

Epilogue

Where do we go from here? We continue intentionally investing in the lives of our children. And you are uniquely equipped to guide your child along their individual journey. With that in mind, I'll offer a suggestion. Write your child a letter, or better yet, a series of letters. It's a way to exercise intention.

Though intentionality takes many forms, one form that has gone out of style is letter writing. Yet, we know the blessing of receiving a thoughtfully written letter explicitly directed to us. As you continue to pour into your children, consider the generational impact of your investment in their lives. With that perspective, write your thoughts, lessons, and dreams on paper.

Your inspiration might come from an event in their lives, whether it be an occasion of celebration or sadness. Your motivation may also come from a thought you don't want to lose. At times it will come from those family stories you always tell. Regardless, take the time to write to your children.

To get you started, I have included a few examples. Read through them. Even read through them with your children. Or better yet, write your own. God has given you all you need to invest in their lives. Go and enjoy them!

When Dreams Don't Pan Out

For my thoughts are not your thoughts,
neither are your ways my ways, declares the
Lord.
For as the heavens are higher than the earth,
so are my ways higher than your ways
and my thoughts than your thoughts.

—Isaiah 55:8–9

Dear Kids,

You've worked and prepared and dreamed. You thought it all made sense. You even thought it was God's will. But it didn't work out. Now what?

But it's not simply "Now what?" is it? There is so much more going through your minds and hearts. Questions seem to be flooding in from all directions. What more could I have done? What signals did I miss? What is my purpose now? Do I have any worth?

Oh, I know the questions. Believe it or not, I've been there—more than once. I've asked those same questions myself. I've experienced the hurt of a lost dream. Now, everything in me wants to take the discomfort and pain away from you. But I can't. And what I am learning, by God's grace, is that trying to take it from you would be to cheat you out of something beautiful.

I know it is hard to see this hurt as beautiful. It hurts, and to deny that pain would be to deny something deep and true. That is not what I mean. Instead, I am speaking of the beautiful work God is doing in you through the hurt.

One thing my theological training and my personal experience have taught me is that the Spirit of God enters our hurt to restore us. In Ephesians 5:26–27, God tells us that Jesus makes His bride beautiful by washing her with the Word. In Isaiah 55:8–9, He tells us that His thoughts are higher than ours. That doesn't mean your dream was terrible, but it does mean that God's way is perfect.

In your hurt, you may not understand what God is doing. I may not understand what God is doing. Regardless, He is good, and His steadfast love endures forever.

I have told you a thousand times that your identity is not in your dream. Now, I want to add something. Your purpose is not in your plan, either. Your goal is to glorify and enjoy God. You can fulfill that purpose because Jesus has entered your brokenness and sin and has restored you to the Father.

No one can take that purpose from you. No one can take your purpose. It will continue to unfold. Abide in Christ (John 15:5) as He continues to unfold His story in and through you.

Through it all, know that my heart bursts with love when I look at you. I hate the pain, but I love what God is doing in you, battle scars and all.

Love,
Dad

Who Are You Trying to Impress?

For am I now seeking the approval of man, or of God? Or am I trying to please man? If I were still trying to please man, I would not be a servant of Christ.

—Galatians 1:10

Dear Kids,

As I thought about writing this letter to you, I wanted to ask who you were trying to impress. I'm not asking that question because of anything specific I see in you but because I know it can be a struggle, and I want you to think about it. At least, that is what I was thinking. But who am I kidding? An equally appropriate question is for me to ask myself is, "Who am I trying to impress?"

You see, I am writing to you to try to care for you. I want to give you wisdom from the ages. I want to provide you with biblical knowledge. All of that is true, but the other truth is that I struggle here too. That's right. Peer pressure, in one form or another, doesn't just disappear.

It shows up when you struggle with wearing the right clothes. You want to ensure you don't look awkward when you walk down the hall. You want to talk to that girl or boy, but you are afraid you will say something stupid. This is not even counting how lesser friends will try to make you fit in by convincing you to do something that goes against your better judgment.

No, I don't worry about those things much anymore. For me, I want people to approve of me. I want them to think I'm intelligent, helpful, and wise. For me, it's easy to stand in front of a room. Sitting across from someone at a coffee table can be challenging. One-on-one is where I find my struggle.

The truth is that seeking approval is not just a teenage thing. It's a human thing. Maybe that thought doesn't encourage you. But be inspired by this. I get it. You need to know something. Your mom and I will always raise you to think for yourself and not follow the crowd. We are trying to raise you not to need the approval of your friends before you decide. We'll always raise you this way, but that doesn't mean we don't know what you are going through. We've been there. Often, we are there now.

That means we can talk about the struggle together. You are a part of a family of imperfect people. That comes as a bit of a shocker. But it's true. That means you can bring the struggle to us. It also means that when I point you to the gospel (as I'm about to), I'm not trying to stick a bandage on a heart issue. I'm trying to encourage you with the truth that it does not change. You and I don't need to seek a man's or teenager's approval. In Jesus, we have the support of our Father God.

Approval seeking was an issue way back when Paul was doing ministry. He wrote about it in Galatians. He had to say some hard things to a church he had planted. They were being swayed by a group of traveling teachers who were trying to tell them that Jesus was not enough by Himself.

Those teachers said they also needed to add their religious works.

Paul wrote to them to remind them of the heart of the gospel. As he did, he made clear that his purpose was to glorify God, not to win the approval of man. That's why he wrote Galatians 1:10. "For am I now seeking the approval of man, or of God? Or am I trying to please man? If I were still trying to please man, I would not be a servant of Christ."

This verse encourages and challenges me, so I'm sharing it with you. You also have my permission to share it back with me. That's how it works when we point each other to the gospel.

Speaking of the gospel, though, Paul keeps writing this letter. You see, Galatians 1:10 tells us that he is not seeking the approval of man. That's good, but the passage sounds like we should be like Paul. It just tells us what to do. But the Bible goes on to tell us how he can live that way. "I have been crucified with Christ. It is no longer I who live, but Christ who lives in me. And the life I now live in the flesh I live by faith in the Son of God, who loved me and gave himself for me" (Galatians 2:20).

Paul can live without the need for man's approval because he knows Jesus loves him and died for him. More than that, he knows that through faith, Jesus lives in him. The same is true for you and me. I know it is hard to live without seeking the approval of your friends. It is for me, too. When you forget, come to me and let's talk about it. We won't stick a bandage on it, but we will look to the One who loved us and gave Himself for us.

Love,
Dad

Mom and I Had an Argument

---

*For where you go I will go, and where you lodge
I will lodge. Your people shall be my people, and
your God my God. Where you die I will die, and
there will I be buried. May the LORD do so to me
and more also if anything but death parts me
from you.*

—Ruth 1:16–17

---

*So if you are offering your gift at the altar and
there remember that your brother has something
against you, leave your gift there before the altar
and go. First be reconciled to your brother, and
then come and offer your gift.*

—Matthew 5:23–24

Dear Kids,

Mom and I had an argument. You could call it a fight, but that would be too strong. We disagreed about something. You heard it. You saw it. You didn't get to see how we worked through it. But you need to know we did. And you need to understand why.

We don't always agree.

Before we get into the making-up part, you need to know this. Believe it or not, Mom and I don't always agree on everything. Shocking I know, but we each have opinions. Sometimes we have the same opinion. Other times, we have different opinions. That's reality, and whatever it is that you think about marriage, you need to know that even the best marriages are made up of two individuals.

It's funny when I think about it, but our likes have blended over twenty years of marriage. We like the same kind of food. We like the same type of vacation spots. We like the same kind of music. That hasn't always been the case. But over the years, we've grown together. Even growing together, we each have our personalities, desires, and wants. At times they clash.

It happens with any two people who spend time in a relationship, whether they are friends, coworkers, or husband and wife. Whatever fairy-tale image you have of marriage, know this. We don't always agree. You won't either. And that's OK because our disagreements are *never* the most critical defining parts of our marriage. We always value one another.

Even though Mom and I have arguments, deeper truths are holding us together. One of those is that we always value one another. Part of respecting one another means we choose to focus on the things we love about each other more than the things we disagree about. That is an important choice we make, but there must be something more to it than that. If we are choosing to focus on the things we love about one another, we're not all that different from a pair of high school sweethearts. If the things we love outweigh the things we don't like, we stay together. No, there must be more to it than that.

We value each other because even on our worst days (and our recent argument was one of my not-so-good days), we know we have been joined together by God. Jesus has loved us, and He is not done with us. And His Word tells me to sacrifice lovingly for Mom and for her to respect me lovingly. It can be challenging. Most of the time, it's a joy. It is always our commitment to one another. We are always committed to one another.

Let me let you in on another little secret. Love is a verb. It is not a feeling. It is an active commitment. And in the worst of disagreements, nothing ever gets in the way of our commitment to one another.

I have a picture of Mom in her wedding dress on the dresser in our bedroom. You've seen it. It was a gift she gave me on our wedding day. Along with her picture, she has written the verses from Ruth that I've given you at the top of this letter. Ruth spoke those words to her mother-in-law Naomi, but they are the most appropriate words to describe our commitment to one another in marriage. They capture the biblical truth and definition of marriage. We may have different personalities and desires, but we are no longer two. We are one.

Our commitment stems from a biblical promise. It is complete. It is without limit. And it is the most important defining characteristic of our marriage. But our commitment is not merely a legal document. The fact of our commitment brings the peace and joy of total freedom within our marriage, meaning we are free to love each other without fear. We are free to disagree without fear that a disagreement will end our relationship. We are free to try to please one another, knowing that sometimes we'll get it wrong. We are free to be us. That's what you do in marriage.

I am telling you all of this for a reason. Conflict is all right. It does not destroy marriage. It is simply a reality of two people who live in a relationship. But reconciliation is always a priority. Jesus taught that in Matthew 5. He even prioritized reconciliation over worship because it impacts our worship.

You saw us argue, and that happens in marriage. You didn't see us work through it. That also happens in marriage. We listened to one another. We listened to what was on each other's hearts. We each confessed to one another the ways we were wrong. We each acknowledged the ways each other was right. Sometimes it gets messy, and some arguments are louder than others. But coming back together is essential. It's a picture of the gospel.

Mom and I can be a mess sometimes. But we are a forgiven mess, which means we can forgive each other. One day, you might be married to someone who is a mess. Value one another. Commit to one another. Find freedom within the bounds of your commitment. And fight for reconciliation. It's worth it. And it's beautiful.

Love,
Dad

A Better Picture of Manhood

Be watchful, stand firm in the faith, act like men,
be strong. Let all that you do be done in love.

—1 Corinthians 16:13–14

Dear Son,

Do you ever wonder what the world would say a guy is supposed to be like? Let me help you out. I think Budweiser captures it in one of their latest ads with the slogan: "Bud Light, the perfect beer for whatever happens next." Those few words say a lot. This little slogan celebrates the idea that the ultimate in being a guy is being available for a party, a good time, a ball game, or whatever. The problem is that in focusing on being available, guys are celebrating passivity. They don't want to plan. They don't want to lead. They don't want to be intentional about the future. They want to be available for whatever happens next.

Now I know that my bringing this up can sound like an old man complaining about the younger generation. Please don't hear it that way. This isn't generational because true manhood is not a matter of age. The truth is that passivity among males is sadly found at any age, which is why I am talking to you about it now. I'm talking about it because I love you, I know you can handle it, and I'm not raising you to be a guy. I'm raising you to be a man.

What's the difference between a guy and a man? A guy is focused on his image with his buddies or the girls. A man knows he is created in the image of God. A guy is focused on making himself happy and getting things for himself. A man knows he is called to care for others selflessly. A guy doesn't want to work. A man knows that part of being created in the image of God is his call to work in God's image (Genesis 2:15). A guy takes it as it comes. A man counts the cost (Luke 14:28). A man plans, submitting those plans to God's design and wisdom (Proverbs 16:9). A guy views a girl as an object or a plaything or someone to serve his interests. A man is called to care for and protect a woman (Genesis 2:15) and ultimately to sacrifice his desires and even his life for his bride (Ephesians 5:25–27). The model for a guy is found in advertising, almost any advertising. The model for a man is found in Jesus Christ (Hebrews 12:1–3).

Son, I am telling you these things now while you are young for several reasons. First, I have raised you to be able to handle these conversations now. We have talked and will continue to talk about important things. Manhood is important. Second, you are bombarded every day with images from the world that would tell you to merely be a guy. Now I don't want you to think I am trying to isolate you from the world around you. I'm not trying to put a fence around you to keep all the bad things out. Instead, I am trying to pour into you to give you a way to see those messages for what they are and to help you engage your friends in a loving and healthy way. Thirdly, you will soon begin getting more interested in girls. I want you to feel safe in bringing your questions to me. Believe it or not, I've been there. Believe it or not, I've learned some things. Believe it or not, I have your best interests at heart. But also know that you need God's Word more than you need to learn from my lessons. I desire to simply walk through His Word with you.

There is another reason I am writing to you, though. We could talk about what it means to be a man and how God's Word gives us a different, more glorious view than that of the world. We'll do that, but when I write to you, I am not merely building into you but to your children after you. You see, you are my son. I am your father. God has given you to me as a gift, but He has also called me to be a shepherd over you and a steward of you. That means that I don't own you. God does (Psalm 24:1). He has given you to me for a season. Through Jesus's saving grace (Ephesians 2:1–10), our relationship will be less like father and son and more like brothers in eternity. I want you to know that I don't only intend to spend eternity with you as my brother; I also plan to spend eternity with generations of sons (and daughters) after you. While it's too much for you to think about now, I am trying to give you a vision for something you will pass on after you.

This seems like a lot to handle right now. Let's keep it simple. I love you with a love you cannot imagine, and God loves you with a love that I cannot imagine. You have a glorious heritage that goes way beyond our family. Your heritage goes back to your being created in the image of God. Instead of listening to a beer commercial about how you should live in this world, let's turn to God's Word. The world wants to tell you to be a guy, and it will encourage you to live up to the slogan: "the perfect _____ [you fill in the blank] for whatever happens next." Instead, let me offer a biblical slogan for your life as a man. This slogan is not dependent upon your age. It goes much deeper than age. It speaks to your heart. "Be watchful, stand firm in the faith, act like men, be strong. Let all that you do be done in love" (1 Corinthians 16:13–14).

My son, be different. But don't be different to be different. Be different for the glory of God. That means you do what 1 Corinthians 16:13–14 says. Be watchful. Be on guard. Do not be passive—stand firm like a rock in what you believe. Do not change who you are to make friends. Anyone who would require that isn't a friend. Act like a man, not a guy. Be strong. That is who you were created to be. That is who you are becoming. And in all this, know that your call is not to try to act macho. But it is to do everything in love because you have been loved. Yes, your family loves you, but more importantly, you have been loved by Jesus (Romans 5:8). And that truth, more than any product slogan, is what I pray will stir your heart to action and to worship.

Love,
Dad

You Are Beautiful

One thing have I asked of the LORD,
 that will I seek after:
that I may dwell in the house of the LORD
 all the days of my life,
to gaze upon the beauty of the LORD
 and to inquire in his temple.

—Psalm 27:4

The heavens declare the glory of God, and the sky
above proclaims his handiwork.

—Psalm 19:1

Dear Daughter,

You are beautiful!
Don't turn away. You are beautiful.
You really are beautiful!
How does that feel? Notice I didn't ask how it sounded.
I want to know how it felt because the reality of beauty and
everything it stirs up inside you runs much deeper than the
sound of words. It gets to the very core of your being. And
that is what I want to talk to you about.

When I tell you that you are beautiful, I notice a slight turn to the side. You are almost trying to change the subject. Why is that? Is it that you don't believe me? Is it that you want to believe me but don't see it yourself? Or maybe, somewhere wrapped up in this whole conversation are the confusing notions of beauty you deal with daily.

A Better Definition of Beauty

Sweetheart, let's start there. We can't walk through the grocery store checkout line without five magazines telling us what to do to be beautiful or, instead, more beautiful. The problem is that those magazines have an ever-changing concept of beauty because the world around them defines it.

There is a better place to look to define beauty. Psalm 27:4 speaks of the beauty of the Lord. It is a truth found throughout the Bible that God is beautiful, that He created beauty (Genesis 2:9), and that the presence of beauty in creation points back to Him (Psalm 19:1). There is another truth in Scripture that makes this whole conversation more personal. You were created in the beautiful image of God (Genesis 1:27). Sweetheart, you are beautiful. You don't need to shy away when you hear it. And you don't need to feel the pressure to run after a lesser definition of beauty.

Beauty as a Worthy Calling

That is true of you. I see it with my own eyes. But I also hear it with my ears. You love music, and one of my greatest delights is sitting at the foot of the stairs and listening to you playing and singing in your room. I know your music pleases you, but let me tell you that there is something deeply and profoundly good in your music.

You see, part of the way you bear the image of God is in your calling and in the things you do. God is beauty, and He created beautifully. When you create, either with music, writing, or the way you decorate your room, whether you know it or not, you are making a statement about God's beauty. He made you that way, and when you beautify, whatever you are beautifying, you bring glory to God.

This week, we were with some friends from church. Both the husband and wife are artistic, and the husband made a comment that spoke to me. He said that when he was converted, even his creativity was enhanced. That is a beautifully true statement that speaks to you directly. Your faith in the God of beauty impacts your definition of beauty and the way you make things beautiful.

One of the things that Mom and I talk about quite often is what you kids will do when you grow up. I, for one, am excited to see what God will do with each one of you. I don't know what it will be for you, but I want you to know that beauty is a worthy calling. I don't mean for you to be a beautician (though that's fine). I mean that whatever you do, bear God's image as you bring beauty to life.

Oh, and another thing. Do you remember how I am always telling you kids to be an influencer rather than being the one who is influenced? That is especially true in terms of beauty. Do not buy into the lies of those magazines in the grocery store. And do not buy into the lie of any man who would change you because he has a lesser understanding of beauty. You are beautiful, and you make the world around you attractive. In doing so, you bear God's image and bring Him glory because you proclaim His handiwork like the heavens above.

Love,
Dad

About the Author

James Dickson (MBA, MDiv) is a husband, father, friend, and pastor. He is a former banker and real-estate developer who responded to the call of full-time vocational ministry where he planted and pastors a church of broken but beautiful people in Trussville, Alabama. His has been a winding journey of coming to see that his identity is in Jesus. While it is a lesson he is still learning, he is thankful to continue the journey with his wife, Anna. They have three grown children: Pierce, Blair, and Stuart. He is thrilled to share lessons learned and being learned along this journey of parenting.

Continue the journey with James Dickson's
A Thousand Little Moments 12-week
small-group study.

www.jamesdickson.org

If you enjoyed this book, will you consider sharing the message with others?

Let us know your thoughts. You can let the author know by visiting or sharing a photo of the cover on our social media pages or leaving a review at a retailer's site. All of it helps us get the message out!

Email: info@ironstreammedia.com

   @ironstreammedia

Iron Stream, Iron Stream Fiction, Iron Stream Kids, Brookstone Publishing Group, and Life Bible Study are imprints of Iron Stream Media, which derives its name from Proverbs 27:17, "As iron sharpens iron, so one person sharpens another." This sharpening describes the process of discipleship, one to another. With this in mind, Iron Stream Media provides a variety of solutions for churches, ministry leaders, and nonprofits ranging from in-depth Bible study curriculum and Christian book publishing to custom publishing and consultative services.

For more information on ISM and its imprints, please visit
IronStreamMedia.com

Printed in the USA
CPSIA information can be obtained
at www.ICGtesting.com
LVHW021338290923
759629LV00008B/126